KEEPING THE SPARK

Alive

KEEPING THE SPARK

Alive

MAKING YOUR YEAR-IN-ISRAEL EXPERIENCE LAST

YANKIE SCHWARTZ

MOSAICA PRESS

Mosaica Press, Inc.
© 2016 by Mosaica Press
Designed and typeset by Daniella Kirsch

Published and distributed by:
Mosaica Press, Inc.
www.mosaicapress.com
info@mosaicapress.com

קהילת בית יהודה צבי
KEHILLAS BAIS YEHUDAH TZVI
הרב יעקב יוסף הכהן פייטמאן
OF CEDARHURST

395 Oakland Avenue
Cedarhurst, NY 11516
516-374-9293
www.kbyt.org

Rabbi Yaakov Feitman
Marah D'Asrah

Avrumi Zelmanovitz
President

Daniel Burg
Vice President

Avi Pifko
Gabbai

Yoel Goldfeder
Secretary

Michoel Greenfield
Treasurer

13 Elul 5775

To Whom It May Concern:

My dear friend Reb Yankey Schwartz has written another excellent book. However, this one is also a *davar b'ito mah tov*. It is both timely and extremely necessary. Young men and women returning from a year or two learning in Eretz Yisroel often have great difficulty adjusting back into life in our mundane often profane world. We frequently recite the well-known posuk in *tehillim* 24 "*mi yaaleh...mi yakum* – "who may ascend the mountain of Hashem and who can remain...?" *Meforshim* explain that it is relatively easy to achieve a temporary spiritual "high" but it is very difficult to remain up on the mountain. Reb Yankey takes returning seminary students and young men leaving their Yeshivos in Eretz Yisrael through the often gut-wrenching process of maintaining their newly found levels of *ruchnius,* while not losing important family relationships and a perspective about where others are in their own spiritual growth. Along the way, he provides valuable advice on dealing with work, internet, *tznius* and other sensitive subjects.

Reb Yankey has done a great service in writing this absorbing and practical book, which is full of telling anecdotes, pragmatic down-to-earth wisdom and many Torah sources for his ideas. I highly recommend this original work and wish Yankey continued *hatzlacha* in all his endeavors.

With great *ahavah* and *yedidus*, wishing the Schwartz family a *kesivah vachasimah tovah.*

Sincerely,

Rabbi Yaakov Feitman

YISROEL REISMAN
1460 EAST 19th STREET, BROOKLYN, N.Y., 11230

Zayin Adar, 5775

Rav Yaakov,

I was delighted to review your new sefer. It addresses the difficult topic of young men and women who return from their studies in Eretz Yisroel, only to find themselves challenged to hold on to their aliya.

We are painfully aware that the aliya achieved in Eretz Yisroel is often lost very quickly. This presents a quandary. Who should deal with this? The Rebbeim and mechanchos in Eretz Yisroel seem to be unequipped (or unwilling) to deal with this adjustment syndrome. The Rebbeim here are rarely contacted before the effects have already set in. It is left to the Talmid to strengthen himself before it is too late. I pray that this sefer will contribute to the necessary awareness, to make this happen.

In a world where many new seforim are published weekly, I am not aware of any other sefer that addresses this topic. Ashrei Chelkicha! May Hashem give your sefer the siyata d'shmaya to fuel a greater awareness of this "yeridah syndrome" and help correct it.

May we make our final aliya to Eretz Yisroel, with a one way ticket inspired by the arrival of Moshiach.

B'yedidus,

Rabbi Yisroel Reisman

ק"ק שער השמים

מרא דאתרא

Rabbi Yosef Viener

71 East Willow Tree Road

Spring Valley, NY 10977

6 Adar, 5775

בס"ד

I am quite pleased that Reb Yankie Schwartz has produced his newest manuscript, "Keeping the Spark Alive." His previous two books provided us with the gift of his insights and wisdom on everyday life. In this, his third book, he has undertaken an important endeavor by providing insight and wisdom for seminary girls on how to navigate the return home while retaining the growth they achieved in Israel. His advice and delicate approach to handling potentially difficult situations is worthy of study. The material herein is easy-to-read, on-target, and of great value. It is therefore a 'must-read' for all seminary girls who want to strengthen their ruchniyos and to 'spark' their continued spiritual growth.

בברכת התורה

Yosef Viener

Table of Contents

Introduction

aruch Hashem the importance of a year in Israel is widely recognized. This is a year of independence, introspection, and personal growth. As we watch the growing community of "post-Israel graduates" we can't help but make the following observation. For some, this year leaves a permanent impression, molding their values and directing their life decisions, while for others it seems to be a "passing phase," a year of fun and inspiration quickly lost and all but forgotten. How, we wonder, can one make sure to belong to the first category?

In this book, Rabbi Schwartz presents a plethora of ideas and practical tools that enable the "post-Israel graduate" to internalize the values and aspirations acquired in Israel and, *im yirtzeh Hashem*, to live by them for the rest of one's life.

The *Mishnah* in *Eduyos* 5:7 relates a conversation between Akavyah ben Mahalalel and his son at the time of Akavyah's imminent death. The son begs, *"Paked alay l' chaverecha"* — appoint your friends to take over your role in directing me spiritually. The father refuses. The son, shocked, asks, "Why not? Have I done something wrong to upset you?" The father answers, "No, you have done no wrong. Rather, *"Ma'asecha yekarvucha uma'asecha yerachakucha"*— your deeds will bring you closer or, conversely, your deeds will distance you. Akavyah is communicating an important transitional message: There are stages in life when your spiritual growth will be mostly directed by role models. But the stage after that is largely in your own hands. Your deeds will either bring you closer or they will distance you from spirituality and closeness to Hashem.

Akavyah's message is pertinent to those who were *zocheh* to be directed closely by teachers and mentors in Israel. Now you are ready for the next stage: "*Ma'asecha yekarvucha, uma'asecha yerachakucha.*" It is your choice and it is up to you. Reading this important book and following its advice is a big step towards taking responsibility for your continued spiritual growth.

Mrs. Dina Schoonmaker
Michlala, Jerusalem

Foreword

"You can live in Eretz Yisrael while in America, too."

The plane began its ascent, and my tear-filled eyes took one last look at the ever-shrinking landscape of Eretz Yisrael beneath me. The only comfort I found was in the brief yet striking message HaRav HaGaon Rav Shach *ztz"l* had imparted to my parents upon their own departure two decades earlier.

After eight years of living their dream in the Holy Land, my parents approached Rav Shach for guidance and direction as to their future. "You can live in Eretz Yisrael while in America, too" was the *gadol*'s unexpected response. Yes, circumstances may force you to leave, but you can recreate your own Israel wherever you may go in the world.

It is only natural for humans to feel an attachment to their home. Away from home, the culture is foreign and the way of life is far from what you're used to. This may be the reason some people never leave their home, and conveniently move around from place to place with an RV, a mobile home. In doing such, one is never uncomfortably away from home turf — you simply take it with you wherever you go.

The Jewish People were bestowed with a most unique gift. Wherever we go in the world, we are able to take our Homeland — our RV — with us. What makes Eretz Yisrael so special is the *kedushah* and Torah seeped into its very essence. Living here is obviously the ideal. But it's often not realistic for everyone. The solution is to take your RV with you, to take the fire and holiness of our Homeland to any place you desire! Regardless of your physical location in the world, you can transform and uplift your immediate environment by taking your candle of inspiration and igniting blazing fires of *kedushah*.

Like everything in life, however, it will require time, effort, and preparation. In the noted *Sefer Nefesh Chayah*, Rav Shimshon Dovid Pincus tells over the story of a man appointed by the Ponovezh Yeshivah to construct a bomb shelter for the yeshivah. He was instructed by the Israeli Civil Administration exactly how to build it. The engineers would drive him mad, constantly changing their requirements and forcing him to replace weaker materials with stronger ones. In frustration, he challenged them as to whether their objective was to build a shelter that would withstand the atomic bomb itself! Their response was immediate: "We want to build an underground shelter so strong that even if there are 500 people inside it, and a bomb falls and blows it a quarter of a mile in the air, it will still land intact."

Our spiritual building requirements are no different. Many of us have had the fortunate opportunity to attend seminary in Israel, utilizing our year to construct a shelter using the strongest of materials — *emes* and *chesed*, to name but a few. If built and fortified sufficiently, the shelter will remain intact even when blown across the world.

This book provides essential instruction and guidance as to how to do just that — take the fire and shelter of Eretz Yisrael to wherever life may take you. And by doing so, even if you are leaving Eretz Yisrael, Eretz Yisrael will never leave you.

Mrs. Rachel Rose, *Rakezet*
Bnot Torah / Sharfman's Seminary

Dedication

Prior to my departure to learn in yeshivah in Israel, my brother, Shmulie, who attended the same yeshivah I was heading to, sat me down and gave me a talk on how to maximize my time in Israel. He explained how yeshivah works there and what to expect from it. He also described our relatives in Israel and what it would be like spending Shabbosos with them. Departing for Israel for only my second time and having never met my Israeli relatives, I was excited and eager to meet them. Over the course of my time in yeshivah in Israel, I spent many Shabbosos with relatives and one in particular stood out as an especially remarkable individual — just as Shmulie had informed me.

Ella Miriam (Peterfreund) bas Chaim *a"h*, fondly referred to as Elimy in our family, was a cousin of my paternal grandmother. She was a resident of Bnei Brak where she lived with her husband and children; one of which was married at the time and lived nearby. She valued family and made a concerted effort to reach out to any family member visiting Israel from overseas, offering to host them as often as possible. I spent many a Shabbos at her home, along with other relatives from overseas, where I got to witness and observe what a special and unique individual she was. She always expressed interest in me and my yeshivah experience and offered guidance and counsel to assist me in some of the difficulties I was going through at that time. As I departed Motzaei Shabbos from her home, she always packed up a bag of goodies for me to take back to yeshivah.

More than her kindness and generous hospitality, her spiritual makeup and focus are what truly stood out. Her home permeated with *kedushah* as the focus was always on the spiritual side of things. At the Shabbos table, she expressed her joy in hearing *divrei Torah* and she shared with me her feelings of pride that her three sons were dedicated to Torah learning — these are just some of the obvious examples of her uniqueness. I remember seeing a copy of Mark Twain's famous essay "Concerning the Jews" taped on her refrigerator. During her final illness, she still attended *shiurim* when she was able to and was always in an upbeat mood when I spoke to her, despite all the hardship she was enduring.

Elimy set an example (to anyone who knew her or met her) of how one should serve Hashem. Her entire life was dedicated to *avodas Hashem* despite its shortness in years. She was a true *bas melech* and *bas Yisrael* of the highest order. Anytime I bring up her name in conversation with someone who knew her, they immediately extol her virtues and talk about what she meant to them. The four children and numerous grandchildren she left behind are a testament to the greatness of her character as they follow in her footsteps and dedicate themselves, each in their own way, to serving Hashem. Her loss has left a gaping void in the lives of the many people she touched.

I am very grateful that my wife had an opportunity to meet Elimy twice and got to know Elimy before her untimely passing. When my wife gave birth to twin girls eleven months after Elimy's passing and a week before her family completed reciting *Kaddish*, it was an easy decision for us to name one of our twin daughters, Miriam, after her.

May the learning and growth the readers gain from this book be a merit for her and elevate her *neshamah* in the *Olam HaEmes*.

Acknowledgments

Writing and publishing a book is a difficult and time-consuming endeavor. During the time I was working on the manuscript for this book, I met Rabbi Doron Kornbluth at an AJOP Convention. As an avid reader, I was familiar with some of the books he authored, but I had never met him in person before. Mosaica Press, at the time, was relatively new in the publishing industry and we discussed their objectives and what they were looking to accomplish. I came out very impressed with what he had to say and made a mental note to be in touch with him as the completion of my manuscript neared. Over a year later, upon the completion of my manuscript and seeing some of the works Mosaica Press had published during that time span, I followed up with Rabbi Kornbluth. Following a number of e-mail exchanges with Rabbi Kornbluth and Rabbi Yaacov Haber, it became obvious that Mosaica Press was the right fit for me to publish this book. It didn't take long for me to appreciate the decision in going with Mosaica Press. The amount of work, dedication, and attention to detail by Rabbis Haber and Kornbluth and the exceptional staff at Mosaica Press far surpassed my expectations. I particularly want to acknowledge the efforts and exceptional editorial work of Sherie Gross, and the beautiful design and layout created by Rayzel Broyde. Chana Devo-rah Sklar, Katie Chana Harris, Daniella Kirsch and Malkie Schuman contributed to the editorial and design processes as well, and their work is no less appreciated. It has been a great pleasure of mine to have worked with Mosaica Press on this book and much credit is due to them for this final product. Nevertheless, any errors or mistakes should solely be attributed to me as the author of this book.

A number of individuals outside of Mosaica Press assisted me as well. My sister, Chani, reviewed the manuscript, provided insight and shared the manuscript with her friends to gain additional perspec-tives and further insight. Rabbis Yaakov Feitman, Yisroel Reisman and Yosef Viener, along with Rebbetzin Minka Bin-Nun, all assisted me in attributing the proper and relevant sources to the material. Racheli Tuchman took the time to review the manuscript and write a review for publication. Rabbi Michoel Green provided insight and assisted in connecting me with people in Eretz Yisrael, who reviewed the manuscript as well. I am tremendously grateful to all of them for taking time out of their very busy schedules to help in making this project come to fruition. Furthermore, I owe an additional debt of gratitude to those that expended even more time writing an appro-bation or foreword for the book including: Rabbis Yaakov Feitman, Yisroel Reisman and Yosef Viener, as well as Mrs. Rachel Rose and Mrs. Dina Schoonmaker.

I have been blessed to have been surrounded by many exceptional individuals throughout my life. My parents have always helped guide me on the right path of Torah and mitzvos and being a parent has opened my eyes to appreciate what a formidable challenge that is. I commend them and I am forever indebted to them for their great ef-forts and achievements in molding me into the person I am today.

Along the way, others contributed and influenced me as well. My siblings have always set an example of what I can become and the mere presence of my children remind me of the importance of always being aware of your surroundings and who may be watching, and ultimately influenced by, your actions.

The importance of maintaining relationships with role models, mentors, and those that can provide *daas Torah* cannot be overstated. I have been fortunate throughout the years to have met and maintained relationships with a number of exceptional individuals who have made a tremendous impact on me. Included in this list are Rabbis Shaya Cohen, Yaakov Feitman, Yisroel Reisman, and Yosef Viener here in the States, and from the Chofetz Chaim Yeshivah in Eretz Yisrael, the Rosh Yeshivah, Rabbi Dovid Chait, and *kollel* member, Paul Laster, along with many friends who have had an impact on me.

Audio lectures were of special help during my first foray into secular society (law school!). The lectures of Rabbi Dovid Orlofsky, in particular, had a tremendous influence on me maintaining — and even elevating my spiritual life — in the secular settings I frequently found myself in.

Spending my life with an exemplary individual who can influence me positively is a blessing that I can never express proper gratitude for. Nevertheless, acknowledging the greatness of my wife, Michelle, and all that she does for me and our children is certainly in order. Devoting herself completely to our children and the upkeep of our home despite society's jaundiced eye toward homemakers is commendable and greatly appreciated. She is setting a wonderful example for our daughters to emulate. Her parents certainly did something right raising such a unique individual and I am forever indebted to them for all that they do for us and for particularly entrusting me with their daughter to set up a home and family with.

HaKadosh Baruch Hu has showered me with tremendous blessings as heretofore acknowledged and all I can hope for is to continue to enjoy and experience the fruits of those blessings. May Hashem continue to shower my wife and me with blessings and allow us to witness the ultimate redemption speedily in our time.

Preface

The Jewish woman is a mystery. She seems to have supernatural power and strength paralleled by none. She is renowned for her perceptivity and sensitivity. She is the pillar of the Jewish home, and thereby, of the entire Jewish People. Jewish history has demonstrated the greatness of a Jewish woman. From mere words of advice to their spouses to beheading an enemy, Jewish women have been a crucial part of Jewish history and in maintaining the nation's holiness. Indeed, Tanach (and other Jewish sources) is replete with events involving women making an impact, and at times, changing the course of history — for the better. The following is a partial list of examples from Tanach and other Jewish sources:

- Sarah Imeinu advising Avraham to evict Yishmael from their home.
- Rivkah Imeinu persuading Yaakov Avinu to deceive Yitzchak into giving him the *berachos*.
- Miriam advising her father, Amram, of his error in encouraging men to separate from and divorce their wives.
- Yocheved and Miriam saving babies from being drowned.
- The women in Egypt maintaining pleasant appearances for their husbands' arrival home from a hard day's labor. The women,

in fact, were the reason why the Jews were worthy of being re-
deemed from Egypt.[1]

- Women not donating for, nor participating in, the creation of
  the Golden Calf.

- Ohn ben Pelles's wife saving him from certain death by not allowing him to join Korach's rebellion.

- Chanah's refusal to give up davening for a child and ultimately
  being rewarded with Shmuel HaNavi.

- Devorah leading the Jewish People as a judge.

- Yael risking her life to kill Sisro.

- Rus sticking to and following Naomi despite all the hardships
  this would entail.

- Esther HaMalkah's leadership and courage.

- Yehudis risking her life to kill Elifornus.

- Chanah and her seven sons sacrificing their lives *al Kiddush Hashem*.

- Rachel convincing Rabbi Akiva to learn Torah.

- Sarah Schneirer starting the modern day Bais Yaakov movement.

- and so many more that I have failed to mention.

There is something unique about the Jewish woman that enables her
to contribute and elevate the nation in so many different ways. There is
an inherent sense of righteousness that guides her words and actions to
uplift the Jewish nation.

It is with this introduction that I lead into the objective of this book,
one that I believe is crucial in order to encourage Jewish women to
"take charge" and help direct the Jewish People back onto the proper
path that we have veered off of.

Contemporary times have brought on a new *yetzer hara* that continues to grow among all sectors of Jews on all levels of observance.

---

1   See *Sotah* 11b. Also heard in a Navi *shiur* from Rabbi Yisroel Reisman.

The internet, blogs, smart phones, pervasive promiscuity in sight, word, and deed, and the mass accessibility of anything and everything a person can imagine available for one to view, read, and absorb. Unfortunately, many of these images, opinions, and articles are creating terrible and irreparable chasms within Judaism. They are breaking up marriages and relationships, destroying *neshamos* and our inherent sense of morality, and challenging beliefs once held to be sacred. So much damage can be done so quickly. The extent of this plague is so widespread that it is difficult to see a solution. Still, there must be one — as we know Hashem always sends the "antidote" before the illness and things most certainly *can* improve.[2]

I believe the best medication and countermeasure to all the symptoms of this great plague is held within the Jewish woman. It is she, the rock behind every man, the stalwart of every family, and the one with a *binah yeseirah* that can "save us."[3] Hence, this book. I have decided to broach a subject that I have not seen tackled in any other book and humbly offer my suggestions in order to help "light the spark." Some of these ideas come from my own experience and have been checked with professionals in the field and others have been gleaned from lectures and articles of others. The goal is to assist Jewish women in strengthening their beliefs, maintaining the growth they have achieved in seminary and sparking the desire for continued growth and further strengthening of their *yiras Shamayim* in order that they elevate not only themselves — but the entire Jewish nation. With proper thought and preparation, the "spark" can continue to shine and light up your life — and the life of those around you — for many years to come!

Yankie Schwartz
Cedarhurst, NY
Teves 5776
yankieschwartz@gmail.com

---

2   *Megillah* 13b.

3   *Niddah* 45b.

Prologue

Years ago, during her year studying in seminary in Israel, my sister, Chani, consistently asked me to come and speak at her seminary. (She even tried to "sweeten the pot," arguing that it would boost sales of my books!) Ultimately, it did not prove to be a practical idea.

Nevertheless, I started to give thought as to what I would say to an audience of seminary girls at the conclusion of their year studying in Israel. As I began to consider the ideas, I realized that the subject is not just "another lecture" or "another subject." Rather, this was one of the most important transitions in these young women's lives, and the potential impact on their homes — and on the entirety of *Am Yisrael* — cannot be overestimated. I began collecting my thoughts on the subject and paid attention to relevant questions and issues that inevitably came up. Over time, it became clear that there was enough material for a book — and a great need for one, too.

As I fondly look back at my time learning in Israel, many positive thoughts come flooding to my mind — as I am sure most people experience when looking back at their time learning in Israel. Most people depart for home with fond memories of their Israel experience, but must overcome the significant and varied challenges to retaining the growth achieved there.

Our focus is on understanding the challenges one faces returning home from a year studying in Israel and how to overcome the adversity when many people, experiences, and events that one may ultimately encounter, challenge and hinder the eye-opening experiences and lessons one absorbed during that year.

Inevitably, the consistent greeting one will receive upon return will be something to the effect of "welcome back to reality" or "welcome back to the real world." It is not uncommon to observe people, upon their return, to have gained a more serious and perhaps, more mature, approach to life, be more religiously idealistic — and sometimes stricter in observance. Often, the intensity of the religious experience fades.

Why does this occur?

Is it preventable?

How can the "transition back to reality" be made smoother and more successful?

We will attempt to address these and other questions in the pages to follow.

The Israel Experience

"Showing gratitude is one of the simplest yet most powerful things humans can do for each other."

(RANDY PAUSCH)

The Israel experience is a unique phenomenon that is the first of its kind in history. Only in the last twenty-five years or so has it become a popular choice and destination for post-high-school students looking to expand their Jewish education and to concretize their understanding of Judaism prior to their next step in life of college, work, and marriage. There is nothing in secular society that is similar other than college students taking a semester or two to study abroad, and that is not motivated by religious or spiritual objectives.

Despite its uniqueness and because of its popularity today, many people neglect to appreciate the significance of the opportunity. It is human nature to neglect to appreciate the good things in life when they are commonplace and/or expected. Nevertheless, it behooves each person to recognize the significant opportunity afforded by spending time studying in Israel. Not everyone is fortunate to have the experience and the experience is not right for everybody, but for those who do pursue it and find it beneficial, it is incumbent on them to recognize and appreciate the opportunity.

A girl taking advantage of the opportunity likely spent the first eighteen years of her life living with her parents and siblings and grew up with her surroundings influencing and shaping her development. Her parents raised and educated her to grow up in a certain manner. They attempted to inculcate all the ideas and lessons they felt were important for her to absorb and utilize in her growth and maturation process. She is now presented, likely for the first time, the opportunity for an extended period of independence while being exposed to a deep level of Judaism she may not have been taught or have experienced before. It is vital for a girl to recognize the importance of her parents in her life and all the sacrifices they have made up until now. Moreover, the financial investment her parents are pumping into the Israel experience and the relinquishing of her presence and assistance in the house are not to be taken for granted. No matter what lessons she picks up and no matter what changes she makes over the year in her religious and philosophical approach to life, a girl must never neglect the *hakaros hatov* she owes to her parents for everything they have done for her, including investing in her seminary experience.

Whether one has never been to Israel before or is very familiar with the Land, experiencing Israel as a seminary student brings an entirely different perspective than one may have possessed previously. She will not be spending the majority of the time there in hotels or touring as she would on a brief trip with family or spending a summer in camp there. This is an entirely different experience. She will be living in neighborhoods — giving her a taste of Israeli society, while spending most of her days attending classes, studying, and involved in *chessed* projects. She will be encountering many girls from different communities throughout the world. It all adds up to provide her with an experience of a lifetime that opens her eyes to depths of Yiddishkeit she likely has never explored.

As the year goes on, she may reevaluate and adjust her priorities and objectives in life, working on strengthening those newfound feelings and beliefs. She will likely have support from fellow students, friends and the seminary staff to pursue the new ideals she has developed. This is all well and good while she is in Israel, but putting into practice all that she has learned and determined to be critical in her life development going forward, is another story. Returning to a society or surroundings that may vary significantly from what she has become accustomed to over the year, presents a unique challenge to maintaining the spiritual growth she has achieved.

More so, a girl that encounters people who disapprove and look to discourage her newfound beliefs and behaviors may face an even greater challenge. No matter what society or surroundings a girl ends up in upon her return home from Israel, she can be assured that the *yetzer hara* will be ready and prepared for battle. Without proper forethought and preparation, the changes she made over the year can become obsolete a lot quicker than it took for her to develop them. Nevertheless, with the proper planning, she will not only overcome the challenges, but will be able to thrive in whatever surroundings she finds herself in.

GETTING PRACTICAL

- Appreciate the sacrifices your parents made for you to go to seminary and express the proper gratitude to them.
- Understand that whatever growth you achieved in Israel can only be maintained if worked on.

Preparing for the Return Home

"Before anything else, preparation is the key to success."
(ALEXANDER GRAHAM BELL)

The month of June has arrived and, no matter how much you may try to avoid it, it is time to prepare for the inevitable — the journey home and beyond.

The lessons and instructions you have accumulated over the past year in Israel are still fresh and finding their ways into the proper crevices of your mind, trying desperately to find a secure place that will ensure they remain part of you. The memories flooding back at uncontrollable speeds give you a sort of rush that urges a smile across your face.

Some questions you may be asking yourself as you begin to pack are:

1. Is your bag overweight?

2. Will you get a window or aisle seat?

3. Will you have room for all the books (and other things) you have accumulated over the year?

Still the biggest question is: what's next?

All throughout life (and primarily in high school), you may have developed plans and ideals for the future; many of which have now fallen to the wayside for a variety of reasons, never to return to the forefront of your mind — or, at least, so you think. You have spent the last year reevaluating and reexamining your ideals and what you want to get out of life. Now you are about to embark on your trip home — to your life. It is exciting, invigorating, and perhaps anxiety-ridden. Because despite the changes you may have made in character, deed, or philosophy, it may have to pass the ultimate test of approval from parents, friends, and peers. In a sense, reintegrating into your previous life, while you have changed, is the most difficult aspect of the return home.

What do you do?

What are you going to say?

You imagine the responses, facial expressions, and perhaps the speechlessness of the people you hold dear and crave approval from. Your thoughts are interrupted by the slamming of the door as your roommate enters and diverts your attention to the last-minute gifts she ran to purchase in Meah Shearim and Geulah. She had almost forgotten to purchase gifts for all her cousins, the mandatory gift for her first-grade teacher who had such a significant impact on her, and the neighbor's daughter whom she once babysat for.

Some may be packing a whole new wardrobe, whether it is inspired by newfound religiosity, weight loss (or gain), or updates in style.

The more important concern is whether one will properly pack her spiritual changes in order that they do not get "squeezed out" by the inevitable encounters with challenges in life. We are talking about the "spiritually craving" new you who has absorbed countless novel lessons, directing your attention to perspectives and motivations you may never have been introduced to before. These lessons are crucial in navigating the waters of life, enabling you to "stay spiritual" while living in a material world.

Many tears will be shed as the goodbyes and farewells are delivered to all those you have developed relationships with. Whether it is Rabbeim or teachers, fellow seminary girls, or residents and families that made you feel at home at their apartments or Shabbos tables, the process of expressing gratitude and saying goodbye can be overly emotional and certainly daunting, knowing this may be the last time you see them for a long period of time.

How do you thank someone and wish them farewell when they made a significant impact on your life and how you view the world?

They may have changed your life goals 180 degrees from what they previously were. Is a mere thank-you, some hugs, and a final goodbye supposed to adequately convey the gratitude you feel toward them?

The best way to express gratitude to a person who makes an impact on you is to give them *nachas* by implementing the lessons they taught you (a nice card doesn't hurt, either!). A parent, teacher, tutor, mentor, rabbinic figure, or anyone in a position to assist another person in their growth, appreciates the process the most when the intended recipient absorbs and retains the lesson. Jewish education is not a highly paid profession. Believe me, they could be making more money doing something else! Educators became educators in large part because they want to help and make an impact. The accomplishment and *nachas* one experiences when the intended recipient absorbs the lesson and implements it into their lives is the ultimate fulfillment and reward for the task.

In other words, if you want to show your appreciation to all those who made an impact on you during your time studying in Israel, visit them in five years. Show them how you not only retained the lessons you learned, but have grown further in the process and are sharing those lessons with others. Stay in touch with them, visit them occasionally to keep connected, and remind yourself of the ideals and lifestyle they inspired you to desire and pursue.

It may sound nice and easy to "stay spiritual" when contemplating the future now, but life is full of distractions and challenges. The return to "reality" will likely make your newly created objectives and goals a lot more difficult to accomplish than what you had envisioned.

> *Chavy was getting ready to leave Israel in a few weeks having had an incredible ten-month experience that opened her eyes to*

a whole new world of ideas and objectives. The realization that it was time to prepare for the trip home had finally hit — and it was difficult to deal with. Having developed new relationships with peers, teachers, rabbeim, and "locals" throughout the year, the thought of just leaving them all behind was overwhelming and difficult to bear.

Chavy recalled similar feelings experienced at the conclusion of a summer in sleepaway camp, albeit on a smaller scale. Still, there was one significant difference. It is easier to stay in touch with friends made in camp and it is likely that you will encounter them the following summer. The conclusion of the Israel experience, on the other hand, may mark the end of a relationship, especially with those that reside in Israel. In order to avoid such a reality, Chavy was brainstorming to figure out ways to maintain the relationships she developed and not let them fall to the wayside as often occurs with long-distance relationships.

Personally, I have endeavored to keep a connection with those in Israel who made a significant impact on me. I call them a few times a year to give them an update on my life and show continued appreciation for everything they did for me (though, of course, it can never be adequately expressed with mere words). Visiting them on my occasional trips to Israel also helps in maintaining the relationships and demonstrating my continued spiritual growth that is, in part, due to their contributions.

GETTING PRACTICAL

- Collect all the contact information of everyone who has had a positive influence on you.
- Write in your journal what you've learned from them, what has inspired you, and what you want to remember.
- Buy them a small gift and write a nice card expressing your appreciation.

The "Phase"

"Do it because they said you couldn't."

(ANONYMOUS)

ou may recall observing friends and family returning from their year in Israel, many of whom appeared to have grown spiritually, as evidenced by their revised mode of dress and pursuit of more spiritually oriented activities. Perhaps they have decided not to go to movies any longer, are more modest in how they dress, or are more cautious with what they say or eat. Boys may be more careful with their attendance at *minyan*. Whatever it may be, the return from Israel often brings changes that are obvious even to the untrained and unfocused eye.

Still, a few months later, many of those adopted changes have eroded or disintegrated and are no longer part of their daily routine. The reversion back to pre-Israel habits will not be as obvious or quick as the adoption of "new habits" in Israel, but you may notice him or her slowly reverting back to previous behaviors, interests, and hobbies. Some of these changes may be normal and expected adjustments to being in a different environment. Some of them are simply giving in to the *yetzer hara*, despite the rationalizations one may invoke to assuage his/her guilty conscious. This type of shifting behavior — the decline — is generally referred to as "the phase."

Some people will not be in favor of the spiritual changes you adopted in Israel (regular prayer, sincere prayer, extra learning, avoiding movies, revised mode of dress — whatever). Some will even be disturbed, but will assume that it is just a phase that the newly minted young adult will get over once reality sets in, in the not too distant future.

Often, they are right. While some maintain their "spiritual high" for a number of years, many "returnees" tend to lose that elevated spirit and almost inevitably come crashing back down to "reality."

If a person wants to prevent "the phase" from occurring, he or she must be adequately prepared to not only face the challenges, but to prepare a strategy to prevent it from creeping up. No one can foresee or envision *everything* they may encounter or that may occur. However, one has a general sense of how her life and surroundings were prior to her departure. This is enough to understand what she will be encountering and dealing with upon her return.

Someone returning home confident in her new approach to life and believing that she does not need to prepare for the return home is an ideal candidate to fall prey to "the phase" and ultimately revert back to her pre-Israel outlook. Even worse, she may develop a disparaging perspective toward the short-lived outlook on life she had developed in Israel.

A number of years ago I observed a young man return from his year and a half away, spiritually uplifted and with a conscious awareness of his Judaism — something he did not posses prior to his departure to Israel. It only took a few months for him to lose it all, as he (seemingly) did not spiritually prepare for his return home and did not devise a plan to protect and maintain the status he achieved abroad. He went back to his old ways and pre-Israel schedule and it wasn't long before he lost whatever elevated awareness he had achieved. Moreover, he developed an acrimonious perspective toward anything spiritually oriented. That perspective continues to evolve into something,

I am afraid, that may ultimately lead him completely off the
proper path of Yiddishkeit.

No one thinks "the phase" will happen to them, especially when the awareness and spiritual sensitivity is so fresh in their minds. Nevertheless, leaving oneself devoid of any protection from outside influences can destroy the spiritual elevation a lot quicker than it took to develop in the first place.

I recently attended a shiur given by Rabbi Dovid Chait, the rosh yeshivah of Yeshivah Chofetz Chaim in Yerushalayim, who made an interesting observation. He asked why did Hashem create a world where it takes time and effort to construct or develop something, but nearly no time to destroy it?

It is a fascinating question — it is a lot easier to lose the inspiration than it took to gain the inspiration. You may have spent the entire year developing inspiration to carry you through life and it can be destroyed nearly instantaneously upon your return home.

I will never forget my first encounter with a returnee from
Israel when I was at a friend's house in the early summer. His
brother, fresh off the plane from yeshivah, would walk around
the house calling everyone in the house "kofers" — heretics —
for participating in activities he deemed to be not kosher.
He too fell off that high perch... seemingly never to return.

The climb up the mountain is longer and a lot more tedious and difficult than the climb down. If you want to remain on top of the mountain and not easily fall off the cliff, plan and strategize in staying strong.

This cautionary approach must be heeded not only by those returning after only one year in Israel, but even those returning home after spending multiple years in Israel. Anyone who gets inspired will eventually get challenged. No one is immune.

Returning home especially exposes people to a totally different environment (sometimes with different morals, different life objectives, and different influences from friends and peers). I have witnessed numerous young men, some of whom spent multiple years in yeshivah in Israel (even those who excelled in Israel and were in the top shiur in yeshivah!), fall from the high perch they reached. Often, they not only revert back to their previous levels, but "go below." A person who was inspired in Israel to reach higher is often the one more likely to fall further than the average person who did not experience inspiration in Israel, and further than they could have fallen without the Israel experience. Why? It is hard to say. Perhaps, they subconsciously, or even consciously, feel the need to rationalize their reversion and distancing from their spiritual high and inspiration, which only leads them to further separate themselves from the Israel experience as time goes by.

Julie grew up in a traditional Jewish family and attended coeducational schools throughout her life. Her upbringing and education stressed a love for Israel and a focus on secular education. Her first exposure to a lifestyle focused on strict adherence to Jewish law and a stress on the inner beauty of a woman was quite an eye opener, to say the least. Her preconceived notions of the perceived inferiority placed on women in Jewish society were completely shattered and an appreciation for the uniqueness of the Jewish woman and her role in society slowly developed over her year in Israel.

Excited to share her newfound realizations with her family, Julie was extremely disappointed by the lack of interest and the nearly vitriolic reception she received upon returning home. She felt that the promotion of intellectual honesty that was a staple of her home growing up was completely ignored when she tried to explain her new attachment to wearing skirts, for instance. The more she tried to "explain," the stronger the reaction and opposition she received, no matter how rational and well-reasoned her attempts to convey her position were.

As time went on, Julie became engrossed in work and school. Her focus on the Israel experience started to fade away and although she knew (in her heart of hearts) that what she had learned during the year in Israel was beautiful and true, it was getting harder and harder to stick to those ideals and implement them into her daily life. Surrounded by "secularly minded" people at home and in her community, her ability to "swim upstream" kept on weakening. Eventually, she was back to her previous self. It was not that she neglected or didn't believe in the elevated lifestyle she connected to in Israel. Rather, she began to believe that to live such a lifestyle outside of Israel was unrealistic and too difficult in today's world, and in society at large. In other words, living spiritually was a fairy tale that was nice while it lasted, but in the real world, it could not survive. In any case, she reasoned, living a life focused on business success and enjoying all that the world has to offer was not a bad thing — as long as she was a good person and performed good deeds without harming others.

GETTING PRACTICAL

- Recognize that there may be people that are not pleased with the "new you."
- Understand that there can be many reasons for the opposition, not all that are obvious.
- Prepare and consult with Rabbanim and teachers on how to deal with the opposition in the most sensitive manner without damaging the relationship.
- Jot down the challenges you anticipate encountering, whether it be from people or the environment you will be returning to.
- Discuss your strategy in dealing with opposition with a Rabbi or teacher to make sure it is a reasonable approach and see if they have any suggestions.

- Prepare to find a Rav, Rebbetzin, or mentor in the community you are returning to, that you can communicate with and look to for advice and assistance in dealing with any issues that may arise upon your return and beyond.
- Record the contact information for friends that grew with you during the year in order to maintain your friendships with them so that you can strengthen each other in difficult times.

Absorb

"Just as food eaten without appetite is a tedious nourishment, so does study without zeal damage the memory by not assimilating what it absorbs."

(LEONARDO DA VINCI)

How can one retain the information, lessons and inspiration learned throughout the year? The first step is to absorb it all into one's very being. It is nice to give thought to all the great ideas and lessons one learns throughout the year and contemplate their ramifications. Still, if the newness is not absorbed properly and developed within, it is all going to slip away rather quickly once exposed to secular society. (On a simple level, it would be similar to a person who gets inspired by a lecture, but by the next day, the inspiration is gone once his attention is diverted to other matters.) The only way to prevent this inevitable scenario from developing is to inculcate the ideas into one's behavior and to consistently give thought to them in order that the manifestation of the ideas eventually become habitual — second nature to one's natural self. Neglecting to ponder the ideas for an extended period of time will likely cause the inspiration to subside. A sponge can lose its moisture by either being squeezed out or left to dry out on its own. You need not only be aware of the environment and society constructively squeezing the inspiration out of you, but must also be cognizant of the possibility of the inspiration drying out on its own if not continuously tended to by keeping it in mind and consistently giving thought to it.

> *The week before the bar exam, I was so steeped in my studies that I had a difficult time falling asleep because my mind would not stop rehashing all the information I went through that day. The fear of failing the bar exam and having to spend another two-month period studying for the next scheduled bar exam was so great that it motivated me to repeatedly review all of the material over and over again. My brain, so to speak, could not turn that process off at night. The information was permeating my entire being and would not let me free myself of it until it all came flowing out during the bar exam.*

This was not about cramming. Anyone who studies for the bar exam can understand and appreciate these sentiments. Nevertheless, if questioned today, I would not be able to recall most of the information I knew so well ten years ago. Attending kollel the following year and working in a non-legal related field ever since, will certainly explain my lack of recall.

Your learning and spiritual connection need to be ingrained to such an extent that it permeates your being; it becomes part of your life. The goal is for our subconscious to naturally lean to the spiritual side of everything. It isn't easy to get to that level, fully, but all of us can get a little closer.

But it takes thought and time.

You cannot wing it, so to speak, just as one cannot wing the bar exam. One must prepare for the ultimate life test of reality and all of its inherent and unintended challenges by adequately preparing for eventualities and situations one will inevitably encounter whether fore-seeable or not. The way to do that (and not be flustered!) is to ingrain Judaism well enough so that whatever may arise, one can spiritually survive and thrive, no matter the challenge.

Nevertheless, preparation on its own is not sufficient to help one stay inspired. One needs to work on oneself consistently, always seeking more spirituality to absorb. One cannot stay strong while remaining stagnant. (An automobile, and a toilet for that matter, runs better when it is used often rather than sparingly.) Work on maintaining focus while constantly seeking out inspiration. Keep learning, attend *shiurim*, and keep in touch with those who grew with you in Israel. It will not be an easy task, but it is extremely rewarding. Also, keep in mind that you can handle anything, as Hashem does not send challenges that we cannot handle.

That being said, "adjusting back to reality" while "staying spiritual" does seem to have extra challenges. In a way, the *yetzer hara* is stronger for those who are more righteous and he gears up to battle the "newly inspired" more than he would ordinary folk. Logic dictates that the greater one becomes spiritually, the stronger the *yetzer hara* needs to be in order to challenge the person.[4] And in today's day and age with countless means at his disposal, it may be easier for him today than ever before. If the absorption of all the ideas you learned and picked up is firm and consistently tended to, and you properly prepare for the challenges ahead, the challenges will be easier to overcome and your ability to retain the spiritual growth will multiply exponentially.

> *Although Esther grew up in a frum home and attended the local Bais Yaakov, she was not prepared for the intellectual and inspirational stimulation she received in Israel. The insights and background into so much of what the Torah and Jewish lifestyle is all about (and the reasoning behind it all) was not the focus of her upbringing and it was quite a revelation to her. Her love for learning and understanding all the nuances of what being a Jew is all about enhanced her Israel experience as she soaked in all that her seminary had to offer.*
>
> *Time flew by and as the days for her return home neared, she was ready and excited to implement all of her newfound*

---

4   See *Sukkah* 52 for further discussion on the *yetzer hara*.

knowledge and lessons for life into her daily routine. The return home was exciting. Still, she hadn't prepared for any challenges. The exhilaration deteriorated rather quickly as the daily grind took over and consumed most of her waking hours. As the days and weeks flew by, the pressures of conforming to society and all its distractions started to wear on her. Although she yearned to live a more "spiritual life," it was getting more difficult to achieve. It was much easier focusing on growth in avodas Hashem *and self-improvement when surrounded by like-minded individuals in school and in Israel, but being "alone" in secular society and the pressures to keep with and strive for success were getting to her. She needed to take time out of her daily schedule to recall what she had learned and focus on the value of those lessons in order to re-inspire herself. Reconnecting and maintaining a connection to her friends from Israel would also be of help. Otherwise, she knew it wouldn't be too long before she would neglect everything that she learned and revert back to her pre-Israel self.*

GETTING PRACTICAL

- Make a list of all the changes you have made or are looking to make going forward.
- Jot down ways that can strengthen the changes you have made and update the list as needed.
- Continue to refer to the list as a reminder of all the accomplishments you achieved and to strengthen your resolve to maintain the improvements you made.
- Stay connected to the friends that grew with you.

Plan

"Plans are only good intentions unless they immediately degenerate into hard work."

(PETER DRUCKER)

"Do not abandon the way of piety, even if you are mocked."

(RABBEINU ASHER — "THE ROSH")[5]

Y ou have spent eighteen years growing up and learning about life prior to your year in Israel. Now it is time to prepare to rejoin that reality. Without proper planning, that world can envelop you rather quickly and influence you into reverting back to your previous ideals and beliefs.

Don't get depressed or nervous! Just as Hashem brought you to seminary, He is leading you back home. You can plan for success! While we can't plan for everything, you usually know the people and places you are going to encounter. You can anticipate who will be helpful, neutral, or even harmful.

Jews are an opinionated bunch. Whether asked to respond or merely presented with information, you can be sure a Jew will have an opinion

---

on what you say or how you behave (and they will make sure you hear their opinion!).

Don't do battle with them! Don't see them as enemies. If they happen to insult you, keep your reactions in check. Most people are good. People deserve your respect, even if you aren't fond of certain parts of their lives. Acknowledge their beliefs and opinions. Remind yourself that there are other valid approaches and one must maintain an open mind and be tolerant of those other approaches. When you change your behavior, it is human nature for some others to feel threatened, or feel you are suggesting that there is something wrong with their mode of life. They may feel attacked. Thus, don't do anything to attack. On the contrary, show extra love and respect. Make it clear that you are doing "your thing" and you think no less of them due to your changes.

The biggest accusation you will likely encounter is that you were brainwashed. For whatever reason, society does not view that term positively and it is solely used to disparage someone who made a change to the dislike of the accuser. It is interesting to note that one who changes his diet, his rooting interest in sports, his major in college, or his life perspectives based on college education is not accused of being brainwashed. It is used as an accusatory and disparaging term against those who one feels is making a religious change not to his liking and in particular, one who decides to be stricter in his Jewish observance.

I remember a student in yeshivah once ask my Rebbi how he should respond to someone who accuses him of being brainwashed. My Rebbi's initial reaction was to respond, "You think my brain doesn't need any cleaning?" Making a change in one's life should not be viewed negatively and anyone who accuses you of being brainwashed is the one who has to deal with the issue because the fact that you changed obviously irritates them. As long as you are not attacking them for what they do and how they behave — which you shouldn't do — then leave it for them to reconcile their issue with your change. If you would have changed your career choice from studying to be a lawyer to studying medicine, you likely would not have encountered the same opposition, if any at all. Thus, it is the "opposing" party that needs to deal with their opposition to your change and there is no need for you to address it.

Part of planning is not just figuring out how to make your family and friends comfortable while staying on your "spiritual high." Part of it is also preparing to integrate back into society. You haven't had many responsibilities during the year and you may have a lot more items on your plate to deal with upon your return home: college, employment, dating, chores at home, etc. Your ability to spend large portions of time dedicated to studying may be hampered significantly and you may encounter many challenges to your beliefs and connection to Hashem in many of the life settings you encounter. Prepare as much as possible for the potential scenarios that may arise so that you can adequately address them.

I learned this the hard way. My naiveté in not preparing for or realizing the challenges I would encounter when I first went out to work was, in retrospect, incredible. I had to navigate important moral dilemmas without much foresight or consideration to the potential ramifications of my decisions. I had to make decisions on the fly — and they ultimately were not always the correct decisions.

My first summer working outside of sleepaway camp presented some moral/religious dilemmas that I had failed to prepare for. I was interning at a law firm and every so often, one of the partners, who was Jewish, would ask me to pick up lunch for him. The problem was that sometimes he specifically requested that I pick up a bagel or pizza at a non-kosher shop. I never even considered declining the request and the only dilemma I wrestled with was whether I should keep my yarmulke on when entering and ordering in the shop.

One of the most difficult challenges I encounter in the business world today is refraining from exchanging handshakes with the opposite gender. I discussed this with my posek when I started working and he felt for me, it would be best to avoid handshakes with the opposite gender. (There are poskim *that permit it in a business setting since it is not* derech chiba, *but my* posek *felt that I should be stringent in this area.[6]) In order to avoid any uncomfortable situations, I try to prepare in advance of a meeting by finding out if a female will be present. If a female will be present, I will reach out to her via e-mail prior to our meeting and explain my practice of not shaking hands. This has alleviated much of any potentially distressing encounters. That does not mean it never occurs, but to the extent one can alleviate a potentially distressing encounter, it would be to one's benefit to do so. I have heard of others who make sure they are holding a drink in one hand and something else in the other in order to avoid the situation.*

The details here are not the point. The point is to think through future scenarios and do your best to plan for them.

Generally speaking, it can be difficult to start something new.[7] In life, when starting a new adventure, a new career, or anything that can be a monumental change from what was previously practiced, one will be anxious and consciously prepare for the new venture. Similarly, one must prepare for the return home in order to be able to retain the inspiration and spark its growth further.

The *yetzer hara* is always on call and in particularly high alert when someone is starting something new that has the potential to elevate or lessen one's spiritual makeup. You may see a convert or *baal teshuvah* experience extreme hardships soon after their changes in lifestyle to a more elevated form. Someone settling in Eretz Yisrael may begin to experience more hardships than they previously did due to the potential spiritual elevation one can achieve there. That may be why Chazal say that Eretz Yisrael is

---

6   As with all halachic issues, each person should consult with his/her Rav.

7   See *Rashi, Shemos* 19:5.

nikneh b'yesurim.[8] Similarly, Chazal refer to Chapter 91 in *Tehillim* (*Yoshev b'sesser elyon*) as a song of protection,[9] which is likely why it is designated to be recited on *Motzaei Shabbos* when starting a new week and when escorting a *meis* out of a *levayah*, as its *neshamah* is moving on to a new stage in its existence. Thus, whenever starting something new, such as a new life back home with a fresh life perspective, one must be on high alert and extremely cautious in her behavior, her decisions, and her overall direction in life in order to shield herself against potential negatively influenced attacks challenging her new lifestyle.

> *Racheli was always one to prepare and be on top of things. Heading to Israel for the year was no different. And after listening to the departing speeches from her high-school teachers and principal, and heeding the warnings of her older sister, she was ready to set off for Israel and entertain new concepts and new ideas and see what may transpire. She was not disappointed by the learning experience as it was everything she expected and more. Being free of most responsibilities and focusing on Judaism was a great experience for her and she knew she would never forget it.*
>
> *As was her personality, after Pesach, Racheli started to prepare herself for her return home and all that it might entail. While many of her friends had supportive families, hers was more challenging. Of course, they were wonderful people and she loved them, but there were potential issues facing her desire to stay "spiritually engaged." From her older sister whose Israel experience was not as uplifting, her older brother who went "off the derech" shortly after returning from his year in Israel, and her family's well-intentioned focus on developing a well-paying career, she had a lot to contend with.*

---

8   See *Berachos* 5a. Also read in a transcript from a *shiur* given by Rabbi Yisroel Reisman.

9   See *Shavuos* 15; *Magen Avraham, Orach Chayim* 239. Also heard in a *shiur* from Rabbi Yosef Viener in his *tefillah* series.

Baruch Hashem, she had friends who were going through the same thing. While in Israel, she made sure to schedule appointments with her teachers and Rabbeim to hear their suggestions. She vigorously took notes at all the concluding classes and speeches dealing with going home and striving to maintain an elevated spirit while returning home.

The day to depart finally arrived and Racheli was confident that she would succeed in her efforts, but she was realistic in recognizing the challenges that would arise. Her arrival home and integration back into secular society was every-thing she expected. The challenges were more overbearing at times than she would have liked or anticipated, but she was prepared for and knew how to handle them as she un-derstood that the challenges were there to aid in her growth. She showed profound respect and love to her parents and went out of her way to be more helpful than ever before. Her parents noticed her great efforts at pursuing her new goals and dreams in life, even if they disagreed with some of them. She found a local Rabbi who helped her and her parents find educational solutions that were acceptable to them all. He helped her focus on treating her parents with proper respect and love, and helped them "let her do things her way." Her siblings felt threatened for a while, but she remained strong — having adequately planned for life at home. Her planning and forethought were really guiding her every step and with the help of like-minded friends, she was succeeding in her efforts. It was not always easy, but her desire and planning along the way has continued to up-lift her and assist her in overcoming the challenges. Every day brings on new challenges, but she knows that they are all part of Hashem's plan and they are all there for her to grow and ultimately reach her potential.

GETTING PRACTICAL

- Write down the potential challenges you may face upon your return home.

- Understand that you may encounter opposition and prepare to be open to the opposition's feelings and beliefs.

- Do not look to attack anyone for their opposition or different philosophical approaches to life.

- Devise a strategy on how to approach and handle the potential challenges and seek the advice of Rabbanim and teachers in refining and approving the strategy.

- Maintain and strengthen friendships with like-minded girls who can provide emotional and intelligent support.

No One Is Perfect

"I am careful not to confuse excellence with perfection.
Excellence, I can reach for; perfection is G-d's business."
(MICHAEL J. FOX)

"Do not do anything that could provoke scorners to ridicule
because those people are in the habit of ignoring the good
things and highlighting what appears evil."
(RABBEINU ASHER)[10]

One of the accusations you may hear is that you are being hypocritical by doing certain things and not doing others. It isn't an accusation one likes to hear and it always seems to sting more than other forms of criticism.

No one is perfect. Of course, you will make mistakes. Of course, you will occasionally look bad. That is life.

Having said that, we do our best to improve in our *avodas Hashem*. The bumps along your path in life are mere bumps and should not completely derail you. Don't get upset if you are accused of being a

---

10 *Orchos Chaim*, Chapter 4, Verse 3.

hypocrite. Brush it off and keep doing your best. Life is not a straight line up and it is unreasonable to expect growth in all areas at the same time, at the same rate. So, indeed, you may be a great "davener" and worse at "judging favorably." We are not machines and growth is organic, long-term, and uneven. That's the way it is supposed to be.

Amy arrived home from Israel rejuvenated and with a strong sense of what being Jewish is all about. Not that she did not receive a credible yeshivah education, but the time away to explore Judaism from angles she never knew existed, inspired her to grow. She arrived home with a greater sense of the importance of what Judaism is all about and the significance of adherence to all its laws and customs.

Amy's family was cautiously happy about her newfound inspiration, concerned that she may look to lead a life down a path different than theirs and subconsciously feeling that she was rejecting their "way of life." Seeing her strictness in observance in excess of how they raised her, raised their concerns as the weeks went by. She felt they were always critiquing her for not cleaning up properly, not spending family time with them as she used to while watching television together, pointing out her deficiencies in her manners, etc. They felt she was being a hypocrite — super-frum in some areas, less so in others.

This obviously was taking a toll on Amy and was not easy to deal with.

Nevertheless, she sought out the guidance of a wise Rebbetzin in her community who was able to guide her in how to behave and react in a sensitive manner to all the objections and critiques directed at her. She saw that there was, indeed, some truth to their assertions (cleaning up after herself, making time for family), and things she could do to improve the situation. The guidance proved to be instrumental in smoothing out the relationship with her parents and allaying their concerns about her behavior. She was able to continue on her path of spiritual growth without permanently fracturing her relationship with her parents.

A law student or medical student would not be accused of hypocrisy for making an error in law or medicine, for people know that they are in the process of working to become an attorney or physician. The same should be true for a girl working on herself to improve her Yiddishkeit. Stumbling and making a mistake does not make her a hypocrite; it makes her human like all the rest of us. However, if she has been spending time critiquing family, don't expect anything else in response! Then, the accusations of hypocrisy may be warranted and justified.

A young lady arriving home from Israel is surely not a polished diamond. Only enduring the inevitable life challenges to her outlook and not only maintaining her status, but elevating it further despite the challenges, produces a polished diamond. Nevertheless, the diamond needs to be polished on a consistent basis in order to retain its brilliance.

Even if she is neutral and never criticizes others' behaviors or outlooks on life, there will be some challenges from others. When you change, people get defensive and can sometimes feel that you are displeased with and rejecting their way of life. Generally speaking, in life, when one encounters challenges, it often means that they are going in the right direction and that the *yetzer hara* is just trying to derail them. Take the high road. Don't be negative and critical at all. Show appreciation and respect, and keep connected in order to achieve your sincere and admirable life goals.

GETTING PRACTICAL

- Be aware of your actions or inactions and pay attention to the criticism as there may be some truth to it.
- Don't act or feel conceited because you changed or are different than others.
- Remember to be humble. The truly great ones possess a great deal of humility and that significantly contributes to their greatness.

Stick to Your Guns

"Stay true to who you are and your moral, core values. Stick to your guns and don't allow other perceptions, assumptions, and judgments to steer you wrong."

(SAMUEL PENNINGTON BAIDOO)

When facing challenges in life, there are certain parameters or red lines one draws that one will not cross no matter what. In attempts to keep proper kashrus observance, for instance:

- A person may be willing to eat salad at a non-kosher joint, but would never eat meat or fish.

- Another may be willing to eat fish at a facility without proper kosher certification, provided the fish has fins and scales, but would never eat meat in the same scenario.

- Others may be willing to eat meat as long as it is not pork.

- And then you have others on the other extreme that would not eat anything without proper kosher certification whether it is gum, salad, popcorn, sliced fruit, etc.

In other words, everyone has their red line that they would not cross.

As with all halachic issues, it is crucial for you to discuss your "red lines" — for who you are now, in this stage of your life — with your Rabbi. Clarity on what you can and cannot do helps everyone involved. What is a basic Jewish law that is a red line and where is there room for leniency? What is simply a stringency?

- Informing your mother that you are not going to eat in her kitchen because she doesn't filter the tap water or does not buy prepackaged checked lettuce guaranteed to be free of bugs, may not be the best approach to take.
- Neither would be telling your eight-year-old brother that he is going to hell for watching cartoons.

It is extremely important to discuss your parameters with an objective outsider, preferably one with *daas Torah*, in order to verify that your approach is reasonable. Having spent the year in Israel, in a different environment, where observance is sometimes perceived very differently than outside of Israel, may cloud one's judgment and impair one's ability to objectively determine what is reasonable in the society you currently find yourself in.

- A guy going to the mikvah regularly may be normal in Israel. However, a young man who never stepped foot in a mikvah prior to his departure to Israel, even on erev Rosh Hashanah or erev Yom Kippur, who now comes home and tells his parents he is going to the mikvah daily is likely going to be perceived as a lunatic (if his family is not Chassidic!).
- A girl who comes home and tells her family she is not driving any longer because it is not *tznius* should probably check with *daas Torah* before making such a drastic decision.

I recall a friend of mine who drastically changed in Israel and wanted to only wear white buttoned-down shirts when he came home. He was smart enough to realize that his parents would feel threatened by this "identity change" and found ways to ensure them he was "normal" and still close to them, while still connecting more to his *"yeshivish* look." (He wore white polo shirts for a while to "break them in"!) The examples are just that — examples. Each of us has individual lives and unique challenges. Speak things out carefully with your Rabbi and don't create division unless it is absolutely necessary.

Nevertheless, the parameters that you do set and determine to be reasonable need to be set in stone. Compromising away from something reasonable may lead you down a slippery slope of no return to a path you did not intend to take. Deciding not to "party" anymore and then going out with your friends to a bar for a night out for old time's sake, can lead you off the path of inspiration and back to the old path you spent ten months divesting yourself of. This can be a very tricky exercise, especially given the sensitivities of those your actions may affect. Thus, I must reiterate the importance of seeking counsel from a wise, objective person — your Rabbi or Rebbetzin.

During my time learning in Israel, one boy in yeshivah, who was doing really well (and avoiding any potential negative influences that would derail his progress), gave into peer pressure one night at the conclusion of a fast day, with a half-day schedule in yeshivah, and went to a place of bad repute. While everyone makes mistakes and we can certainly recover from them, this particular boy was never able to recover. He started going out regularly and his learning suffered. If it happened during the Israel experience, it can certainly happen to someone in a more open and secular environment. No one is immune and that is why it is so important to draw lines and to not cross them.

> It had been only two weeks since her arrival home, but Sara was feeling the pressure already. She wanted to stay strong in her ideals, but the challenges were significant. Whether it was a college professor assigning an inappropriate book to be read, her boss asking her to purchase food for him at a non-kosher establishment, non-religious relatives requesting she participate in mixed dancing at a relative's wedding, or old friends ridiculing her for not willing to go to the beach anymore... this wasn't going to be easy. Sara started to question

herself and wondered whether she was strong enough. She began to feel like the whole world was against her. She didn't know where to turn for help.

Debbie had determined that it would be very important for her to be shomer negiah *upon her arrival home, despite the fact that she had not been careful about this restriction prior to her year in Israel. Little did she realize the extent of difficulty this undertaking would be. The bewilderment (and, sometimes, lack of respect) on the part of her family and friends, took her completely off guard. Also, she realized that this was only the beginning of what was yet to come. Once she would start college and start working in a secular environment, the challenges were certainly going to multiply. The mere thought of it was causing her great anxiety. She hadn't realized how difficult this was going to be. All she wanted to do was to return to the safe confines of her seminary where she enjoyed protection from all the challenges she knew she had to face in the secular world.*

No matter what you (and your Rabbi/Rebbetzin) ultimately decide to use as a guideline and the parameters you set up for yourself, the challenges will be there to compel you to reconsider your decisions. Whether the challenges begin immediately or only arise months later, they will be there and it will be difficult to avoid "bending" the rules.

Change brings challenges. It is similar to someone taking on something new before Rosh Hashanah or *lehavdil*, a non-Jew making New Year's resolutions. How many people end up keeping to those resolutions? It isn't easy and everyone needs help, but you will, *b'ezras Hashem*, be able to withstand the challenges. Whatever commitments you have made, strengthen them and stay committed. One "slip" can lead you down a slippery slope. On the other hand, don't be nervous if you slip. We are human. Still, understand the gravity of the slip so that your dedication to the cause you deem important is strengthened to a greater level than before.

GETTING PRACTICAL

- Put together a list of decisions and changes you wish to adhere to.

- Review them with your Rabbi/Rebbetzin to ensure they are reasonable, both halachically and hashkafically, given your background and the surroundings you are returning to.

Torah Learning

"He who does not increase his Torah learning decreases it."

(HILLEL)[11]

You have spent the past ten months learning Torah, including many subjects you may not have broached previously. You have listened to lectures and attended classes from teachers and speakers, the likes of which you may have never encountered before and will likely not encounter again. You have delved into previously learned subject matter as well as subjects you may never have learned before at depths you likely were not familiar with. It has been an awesome, exhilarating, and uplifting experience, to say the least. Now you are heading back home and likely will not be attending a seminary any longer where you can be exposed to learning on a consistent basis.

How do you retain some semblance of the learning and studying you accomplished over the past ten months? Furthermore, is it necessary?

In today's society with women of all backgrounds attending secular institutions and joining the workforce, it is vital for them to stay connected to spiritual resources such as learning, attending lectures, and developing relationships with spiritual mentors. Being exposed to secular society for

---

11   *Pirkei Avos* 1:13.

a large part of the day, devoid of any spirituality, can be harmful to any person. Although men may have the obligation to learn, women should not avoid it as society continues to evolve and shares more of the previously male-centric duties with females. Women share the same exposure as men and although, spiritually speaking, women may be inherently stronger, they are not immune to outside influences.

It is extremely important to keep pursuing learning and not to give it up completely. Jews can only grow if they are learning. Indeed, without learning, it is impossible to grow. The lessons learned throughout the year will only stay with you and manifest itself in your actions, if and only if, there is continued learning and a consistent pursuit of growth. The same way one will not remember her studies on subjects she no longer pursues or may forget previously learned ideas that she is no longer contemplating or exposed to, this can occur to Torah studies as well. Parents will experience this when assisting their children in *parashah* studies if they haven't studied the *parashah* since they were in a yeshivah. No matter how well you may know something, losing exposure to that subject matter and neglecting it in your thoughts will eventually lead to the erosion and loss of the ideas and lessons gleaned from that subject.

> *Chani was still flying high from her Israel experience through the summer and into autumn, but after the conclusion of the Yamim Tovim and having to work full-time and attend college at night, she was finding it very difficult to maintain a learning seder on a consistent basis. Learning with friends was almost impossible as everyone was running on different schedules. Even trying to find time to learn on her own was proving to be more difficult than anticipated, as she was spending many evenings investigating shidduchim and setting up dates for herself. The amount of time needed for all her work, schooling, and dating left no time for any spiritual endeavors and it was starting to impact her. Without the exposure to learning, outside secular influences were having an easier time penetrating the spiritual barrier she worked so hard on erecting over her time learning.*

Her schedule did not allow for her attendance at lectures and when trying to learn on her own late at night, drowsiness and sleep usually prevailed. In order to prevent her whole spiritual life from spinning out of control and losing it all, she determined that she needed to start focusing on finding time for her learning. At the beginning of each week, she put together a schedule that prioritized her learning and made sure to never neglect it. No matter what was in store that week, she knew that time set aside for learning could not be compromised.

Setting aside time to learn consistently may be one of the most difficult tasks to keep going after Israel, but it may be the most significant task in retaining your spiritual elevation.

In his pamphlet entitled "Reflections of the Heart,"[12] Rabbi Shaya Cohen states the following:

When the Torah was given on Mount Sinai, first the women were taught everything and only later, the men. Rabbeinu Yonah explains that in reality, the women are those who are responsible for the future of the Jewish people. It is the mother who will implant the most basic values and sensitivities, and develop the emotional stability of the child at the most tender years. It is this which is in reality most fundamental in the continuity of the Torah for the generations. It is these values, sensitivities, and this stability which enables the child in future years to take part in that great heritage which comes to him from his ancestors, to further it and to pass it on to those after him. It is the major portion of this responsibility that the Jewish mother bears and therefore, the women were taught the Torah on Mount Sinai before the men.

A wife that pursues spiritual growth by attending *shiurim* and learning from a *sefer* or book can better relate to her husband and his desire

---

12   Published by Priority-1, 2006.

and drive to learn. Seeing his wife sharing a similar pursuit in striving to grow spiritually will also influence his drive to learn. Children seeing their mother prioritize spiritual growth will seek to emulate her actions. In other words, learning will not only enhance your own spiritual makeup, it will improve your relationship with others and make you a better role model. The one thing my grandmother remembers about her father and that she consistently conveys to me is that she always saw him at home with a Gemara in hand. As a child spending Shabbosos at my grandparents' homes, one of the things that I saw that made an impression on me was seeing my grandmothers daven Friday nights at home, attend shul Shabbos morning and attend Torah lectures in the afternoon. Continuing to grow and actively pursuing spirituality will inevitably make you a better *mechanech* for your children since actions generally make greater impressions than mere words.

GETTING PRACTICAL

- Set up a learning schedule and stick to it; whatever it may be. It may be attending classes, studying with a learning partner, watching lectures online, to name a few.

Avoidance

CONFRONTATIONS, HALACHIC AND HASHKAFIC BATTLES

"Do not act as if you were superior to others, on the contrary, be humble as the dust that everyone tramples underfoot."

(RABBEINU ASHER)[13]

Rabbi Yisrael Salanter is quoted to have said that he first tried to change the world, but realized he couldn't do it, so he focused his efforts on his city. When he realized he could not influence his city, he set his sights on his community, but that still did not bear any fruit. He then pursued influencing his family and that too, did not meet with success. He finally realized that his focus should solely be directed at his own growth.

The same is true with all of us. You may think you are going to come home and change the world. Before focusing on the world — or your family — focus on improving yourself. If you focus on "helping" everyone else in your life and neglect yourself, even your own growth

---

Orchos Chaim, Chapter 4, Verse 14.

will be hampered. This is not to say that one should not pursue *kiruv* or some other path to make an impact on others, but all other pursuits should be secondary to focusing on maintaining your own growth. First, make sure you are grounded before pursuing making an impact on and influencing others. It may take six months or a year — or even more — for you to get re-acclimated into society and strong enough to withstand the challenges of "living spiritually" in a new/old environment. Don't worry, it is doable and you'll be able to affect others as well, eventually.

With your newfound halachic and hashkafic knowledge, you may quickly discover that many Jews — perhaps, including those close to you — are not necessarily "doing everything right." Sometimes, their priorities are simply different than yours, and each way has its own validity. Sometimes, there are objective problems.

Don't judge people. Don't try to change people — especially your family! Don't challenge them.

No one likes change and certainly no one likes it when someone else tries to change them, for it is perceived as an adverse judgment against one's chosen lifestyle. It is human nature to get defensive and not appreciate admonishment and rebuke for something a person has been practicing all his life.

> *Shani was a perfectionist by nature and demanded the same from others. Being the oldest of five children, she was accustomed to mentoring and teaching her younger siblings the correct way to do things. Having recently returned from a year of studying in Israel with a newfound perspective on adherence to Jewish law, she was on high alert to critique and correct her siblings' every action. From tying shoes to cutting nails, from reciting proper* berachos *to going to shul on time, from proper speech to proper* middos, *Shani was all over the map in pointing out everyone's shortcomings and it certainly wasn't going unnoticed by her siblings and parents. Her criticism was alienating her from her family and their excitement for her newfound maturity and perspectives on*

life quickly waned, to be replaced by animus toward her and her never-ending criticism. If not for her friends noticing the chasms she was creating by her drive for perfection in others, and pointing it out to her and helping her correct it, she could have created irreparable damage between herself and the rest of her immediate family.

Everyone is entitled to choose how to live their lives no matter how much we may disagree and think to the contrary. It is common for the recipient of criticism to view the offending party as pompous and conceited, irrespective of who is right. There is nothing to gain by confronting others.

Of course you are coming from a good place. There is a natural urge to share newly discovered ideas that one finds to be enlightening. Upon your return home, you are most certainly going to possess the urge to assist and enlighten others to realize the "true and enlightening" path you have discovered. Even though your intent is genuine and admirable, you must resist the urge to preach and share all the new ideas with others. One of the keys to be effective in *kiruv* is that the intended recipient must be open to listening. Without an open ear, no matter the words said, the energy exerted, the extent of the efforts and the intent of the *mekarev*, it will all fall on deaf ears and will not be appreciated. Avoid efforts in preaching and proselytizing. Focus on your own growth.

The greatest impact is usually made by setting examples. Let others observe your behavior. If they appreciate your sincerity and see what the "new you" is, that will impart the message more effectively than any active pursuit you wish to take to influence others. The same way a parent or a mentor's actions many times can influence children or a student more than any statements, the effectiveness in effectuating change in others (whether it is someone older, a sibling, friend, peer, or anyone else), will be higher by setting examples with your behavior and actions and it may be the best potion to achieve your goals.

A key to success in life is learning to ignore things we see, even things that need correction. Don't pay attention to everything you see. Sometimes, it is good to ignore something and not to delve into a subject or idea the other party has no interest in discussing. If your mother does not cover her hair or is not particular about avoiding foods with bug infestation, your father is not particular in checking new clothing for *shaatnez*, your sister does not adhere to proper *tznius* guidelines, or your brother thinks it's okay to text on Shabbos, don't point out the error of their ways.

Focus your attention on avoiding potential problems. Prepare the food yourself so you do not have to be concerned with any bug infestation. Delicately mention to your father that you are taking something to be checked for *shaatnez* and offer to take his new suit (if he isn't interested, don't ask again!). Don't criticize or try to change them. Many things can be done without the other party realizing it. You can purchase a hat as a gift for your mother. You can take your sister shopping for more modest clothing without informing her of your intent. You can keep your brother occupied on Shabbos so that he doesn't have time to text.

No one likes rebuke. It almost never works, and it almost always causes resentment. I have observed on numerous occasions, newly minted young adults, upon their return home from Israel, take an accusatory path nearly as bad as accusing their mother of being *mechallel Shabbos*, their father of not keeping kosher, and their siblings of essentially being "*goyim*." The rationale behind the accusatory statements may be accurate — although often they aren't — but the accusations are never going to be received well. No matter how tactful your approach is, do not even consider it. The act of rebuke is never well-received. If others' behaviors may impact you, you need to figure out a way to avoid the result of their actions without attacking them. Remember, everyone is on high alert around you so anything you say will be assumed to be an accusation of doing something wrong. Try to plan as much as possible to avoid any situation where you will have to explain to somebody why their actions are to your disapproval.

GETTING PRACTICAL

- Even if you do not have political aspirations, prepare and learn to be diplomatic.
- Avoid confrontations.
- Learn to not see everything.
- Think of ways to prevent a situation devolving into something you will disapprove of.

Your Room Should Be a Sanctuary

"In the private sanctuary of one's own conscience lies that spirit, that determination to cast off the old person and to measure up to the statue of true potential."

(THOMAS S. MONSON)

No matter your surroundings and exposure to outside influences, one place that is crucial to keep protected from such exposures is your room. Everyone needs a place that they can go to let out steam, a place to have privacy to feel relaxed and comfortable. We all need a "safe place" to enable us to take time and contemplate life. In today's society with the innumerable and incessant distractions available to even those not interested in pursuing, it is extremely difficult for one to have time to just process everything and consider all that was observed and experienced. Spend a few minutes observing people in public: how long will it take for you to see someone looking at their phone?

You know how people feel uncomfortable in the dark and in isolation? Nowadays, people feel uncomfortable standing without anything to do — so they inevitably look at their phone every few seconds. Can you imagine what a creature landing on earth would think when observing people continuously glancing at a small electronic device every few seconds? Nevertheless, that is society today. Who takes time for themselves to just think about life and what they are doing? Life is so much nicer, deeper, and calmer when we can "step aside" from the chaotic everyday happenings every once in a while to consider the big picture. All the distractions are ultimately a means utilized by the *yetzer hara* to keep one too busy to stop and consider the big picture.

If you live in a home that is more liberal in its approach to life relative to religious observance, having your sanctuary separated from television, internet access, and inappropriate speech, for instance, is vital. If you share a room with someone whose outlook on life differs vastly from yours, find a safe place that you can frequent and be free of distractions in order to have time for in-depth thought. Alternatively, arrange to be in your room alone on occasion or use headphones to listen to an inspiring *shiur* — blocking out the world.

> When I was in law school, especially close to exam time, I used to take an hour lunch break and go to the local park near school to take a break from my studies. During that limited time, I could enjoy nature, think about life, and listen to a Torah shiur. Those times saved me. Similarly, when I worked as a summer intern at a law firm, I would walk to the nearby Twin Towers, where there was a lovely water spring and an area for people to sit and enjoy the summer weather while taking in the scene.

A full-time worker can do the same. Take some time out of your day and examine the big picture of life.

Women don't have the same requirement to daven with a *minyan*, but taking time to daven, learn, and reflect upon the big picture of life will assist you in breaking away from the chaos of everyday life. It will enable you to continue to pursue personal growth to whatever extent possible with the limited amount of time available.

Time is life and every second wasted can never be regained. Dedicate time daily for personal growth and ideally set aside a place to act as your sanctuary.

Aviva came from a large family with both of her parents working full-time to adequately support their large brood. With not much room in their small house for self-reflection isolated from others, she felt the need to find time to herself after spending much time reflecting on life during her year in Israel. After giving it some thought and consulting with someone whose objective opinion she respected, she decided it would be best for her to dorm in college in order to focus on her studies and to find time to herself to enable her to continue growing spiritually. She went home for most Shabbosos and tried to use her days off from school to find a quiet and serene area to connect to G-d and just reflect upon life. Many years later, with a large family of her own, she fondly recalls those times of self-reflection and considers them to have been vital to her spiritual growth and the person she has become.

GETTING PRACTICAL

- Make sure to schedule down time for solitary reflection.
- Find a place where you can get away from everyday distractions if such is not available at home.

Names

"What's in a name? That which we call a rose by any other name would smell as sweet."

(WILLIAM SHAKESPEARE)

Many people give thought to change their preferred name from secular to Hebrew. Hebrew names are holy and have intrinsic meaning. In fact, a name can actually reveal a person's characteristics and essence.[14] The Midrash[15] says that when Adam HaRishon was naming the animals, he looked into their essence and named them accordingly.

The intention to use your Hebrew name is wonderful, but it is not always the wisest decision. Aside for the potential for embarrassment for someone with an unusual or peculiar Hebrew name, one may rankle the feathers of those who are used to referring to you by your secular name. You may bring undue pressure and adversity upon yourself by taking such a path, and it may not be important enough to warrant the discomfort. Again, I must reiterate the importance of having a Rav/

---

14   See *Berachos* 7b; Arizal, *Shaar HaGilgulim* 24b.

15   See *Bereishis Rabbah*.

Rebbetzin to discuss sensitive matters with, to guide you on the right path, and advise when it is worthwhile, if ever, to go down the path knowing attacks will be forthcoming.

> *Michelle was always fond of her name, given its popularity in secular society and sharing it with many popular stars and entertainers. Besides, her Hebrew name left much to be desired, especially since her family could not even pronounce it. Michelle fit in with the rest of her family, all of whom went by their secular names, with many of them not even knowing their Hebrew names to begin with.*
>
> *As her time studying in Israel was coming to a close in the not too distant future, she started giving thought to her Hebrew name and its significance. Having spent most of the year learning about Judaism and all it has to offer, one of the changes in her lifestyle that she was contemplating implementing was switching to her Hebrew name. Not wanting to cause too much friction with her family upon her return home, she wisely went to discuss her dilemma with one of her teachers in seminary whom she had developed a strong kesher with and whose opinion she valued and respected. Upon discussing all the details of her family dynamics and the potential friction that changing her name may create, her teacher advised her to keep her secular name, at least until she gets married. It would avoid unnecessary friction and minimize the expected challenges she anticipated having to deal with upon her return home.*

GETTING PRACTICAL

- Before considering changing the name you are referred by, speak to someone with objectivity who can assess the dynamics of the situation and the impact such a change would have.

Peer Pressure/ Friends

"It is curious that physical courage should be so common in the world and moral courage so rare."

(MARK TWAIN)

"Be a loyal friend to those who fear G-d, attach yourself to them; avoid the company of evildoers, and love those who reproach you."

(RABBEINU ASHER)[16]

T he Israel experience is generally considered a positive experience. You may go with many friends or just a few, but oftentimes is the case that you are likely to make new friends as well. Many may grow along with you while others may stay grounded in their pre-Israel perspectives and approach to life. Some may even "decline."

Orchos Chaim, Chapter 2, Verse 7.

Whatever the case may be, you are eventually going to go home and may face a number of different challenges from many different angles, one of which may be that of peer pressure. Peer pressure can come in many shapes and sizes. From actual friends, classmates, work colleagues, and the like, you are going to find yourself in situations where your contemporaries are going in a direction that you do not want to be part of. Some things may be easier to avoid or decline than others, but there will be a point at some time or another, when your scruples are going to be challenged.

Ruchama was excited to start her career at a well-recognized firm of excellent repute. She had overcome a lot in life to get to where she was and to finally be earning a respectable salary felt like a great achievement. Little did she know that a whole new set of challenges were lying in wait.

It had always been her dream to join corporate America, having been brought up to strive for and appreciate success in school and ultimately at a career. She had come across a number of bumps along the way, but always managed to circumvent and overcome the hurdles. Her greatest hurdles were yet to come though.

At first, Ruchama thought it was a great setup to be assigned to a department with other Jewish employees, but she quickly realized how wrong she was. The many nuances in halachah that she picked up during her year in Israel and instituted as part of her daily living were being challenged on a constant basis by her peers who were all seemingly more lenient in the way they incorporated the nuances of halachah into their lives. From decisions on how to deal with attending meetings at non-kosher restaurants to being surrounded by colleagues proficient in foul language and abusing their privilege of speech, Ruchama had many obstacles to consider in navigating the pressures of her secular work surroundings. She couldn't just say her religion precluded her from certain activities when her fellow Jewish colleagues had no problems with those same activities.

Ahuva had built up a strong circle of friends over the years hav-ing spent most of her life with a select few whom she attended school and camp with. During vacation and off times, they would enjoy time at the beach, swimming, and other fun activi-ties. They all went to Israel together with the idea that it would be great to get away for a year strengthening their bond before attending college and having to get serious in life. Although they all planned on gaining from their Israel experience, they all did not grow and gain at the same rate. Ahuva seemed to have taken on a whole different perspective than many of her friends had, but there were two, Leora and Meira, that grew at the same pace as her. Upon their return home, Ahuva's ability to avoid and decline some of the rendezvous with her friends that she deemed to be inappropriate was strengthened by the fact that she had two friends agreeing with her and supporting her posi-tions. When push came to shove, she knew she had the support of Leora and Meira and that gave her the strength to stick to her newfound convictions.

Whatever the case may be, it is important that you have a group of friends that are on the same page as you. One can more ably over-come challenges when part of a group as opposed to as an individual. Sharing the same philosophy as others will strengthen your beliefs and conviction to pursue your goals. If you are the only one battling peer pressure at work or school, your resistance to the pressure may be weaker than if you had friends battling the same pressure as you. Invest in friendships that will enhance your spiritual growth and the returns will be invaluable.

Rabbi Chaim Volozhin explains in his *sefer*, *Ruach Chaim*, that the statement in *Pirkei Avos* to "acquire for yourself a friend" is in order that you have someone to look to for advice on moral issues.[17] I heard Rabbi Yisroel Reisman explain this to refer to situations where a person does not feel a Rav could adequately advise him since he believes that a Rav lacks exposure to the outside secular world. A *yeshivah bachur* that leaves yeshivah to go to work for his father and discovers his father doing things that are not "kosher," may find it difficult to discuss this with a Rav. He knows the Rav will advise him not to do anything not kosher, but the *bachur* may have been planning to take over the business. Now what does he do? A friend, on the other hand, who may have had a similar experience, can advise him on how to avoid anything not "kosher" and strengthen his resolve to stand up to anything he shouldn't be doing since his friend may have succeeded in a similar scenario.

GETTING PRACTICAL

- Make sure to keep in touch with friends that are on the same page as you observance-wise.
- Keep up with them, stay connected, and try to meet up with them as often as possible.

---

17   *Pirkei Avos* 1:6.

Maintaining a Connection

"Physical attractions are common, but a real mental connection is rare. If you find it, hold onto it."

(ANONYMOUS)

One of the key aspects in maintaining the growth that you have gained over the year and continuing to grow further upon your return home is to maintain a connection to the Israel experience. Whether it be keeping a *kesher* with teachers, the seminary, or *madrichos*, or continuing a dialogue with someone who made an impact on you while in Israel — all this will help in maintaining and continuing the process of growth further.

They know you and will be helpful in helping you to continue to grow and navigate the challenges of life. Moreover, just the reminder of what you learned and how you felt during your year in Israel can trigger emotional feelings and the desire to grow further just as you did in Israel.

Dina had a great experience in Israel and was determined to cultivate the relationships she had developed in Israel, including the teachers she had gained a respect for and looked to for guidance throughout the year. Little did she realize how difficult that would be given the seven-hour gap in time in addition to the busy schedules of all parties, including her own. Nevertheless, she was determined to make it work and she made sure to consistently reach out to her teachers and enjoyed the conversations she had with them despite their brevity and lack of consistency. The relationships came in handy when unexpected challenges arose and she needed someone to discuss them with. Additionally, whenever she felt down or depressed, just talking to her teachers lifted her spirits even if they could not help her with a particular challenge.

In today's day and age, it is a lot easier to keep a connection with people no matter how distant they may be.

During my time in Israel, I took long walks during lunch break and after night *seder* in order to get some fresh air, stay in shape, and take a break from the rigors of a full day of yeshivah study. During those walks, I would think about life, dream about my future — all while listening to music. Little did I realize that those music sessions would come to be very handy.

Much later, I discovered that whenever I would listen to those same songs, it triggered memories of Israel. In researching the idea of memory being triggered by music, I came across a research paper online that discusses many sources to support the idea that music can trigger certain memories and as a matter of fact, it cites a book published in 2007 that delves deeper into the sources and the seeming connection between memory and music. Not only did particular songs trigger memories of my Israel experience, they actually brought me back to a particular place or experience where I listened to that particular song.

For those who enjoy listening to music, that activity can also assist in maintaining a connection to the Israel experience.

It has been over fifteen years since I departed Israel for home and I continue to maintain a relationship with the Rosh Yeshivah of the yeshivah I attended. I called him annually for many years before Rosh Hashanah before he started spending significant time in New York, where I make an effort to meet with him. I developed close relationships with some of the *kollel* members of the yeshivah and have continued a correspondence with them over the years. I also try to keep in touch with my family in Israel that I got to know during my time there. The easiest way for me to remember to reach out to them is that I always try calling them before or during a significant time on the Jewish calendar.

Do not discount the significance of such connections. It will be a strong drive of your *yetzer hara* to separate you from the Israel experience and distract you from thinking about it as much as possible. The more distractions you encounter in your daily lives, the many activities you may be involved with between family, work, and friends, and the continued expansion of the distance from your experience in Israel will all impact and impair the spiritual makeup you created in Israel. Any means of maintaining and strengthening that connection and disrupting or halting the continued distancing from the Israel experience will enhance your ability to hold onto and ideally, strengthen your grasp, on that experience.

> *Shoshana could not believe that three years had already passed since her arrival home from Israel, but seeing her sister, Elisheva, three years her junior, off to Israel only confirmed that fact. It had been quite a whirlwind experience over the last three years, trying hard to maintain the spiritual growth she achieved in Israel. Cultivating and sustaining relationships with those who influenced her in Israel was a key aspect in preserving the connection to the Israel experience that inspired her to hold on to and expand her growth despite all the challenges. And it was only fitting for her to share the contact information for those people with Elisheva so that she too could develop relationships with those same spiritually elevated individuals.*

GETTING PRACTICAL

- Create a directory of those you developed positive relationships with in Israel and record their contact information.
- Make sure to reach out to them occasionally. Keep a calendar to track the correspondence if you need to.
- Share your contact information with them so they can reach out to you as well.

Shabbos

"Shabbos invites all those who need new energy, all those who have been broken by the world of the six days, who need the world of Shabbos to make their brokenness whole again."

(SHLOMO CARLEBACH)

One of the greatest gifts Hashem bestowed upon the Jewish People was the day of Shabbos. As it can be with many things in life, Shabbos is sometimes difficult to appreciate at a young age, but as one gets older, we can appreciate the gift a lot more. With "modern chaos" seemingly engulfing our natural daily routine and something we have become accustomed to, a day off presents a relief welcomed by all. Nevertheless, as a Jew, it is an opportunity to focus on and excel in other elements of life, primarily the spiritual side.

You likely spent the last ten months in Israel focusing on the spiritual aspects of life. To shut out spirituality now due to all the everyday involvements you find yourself busy with, would be jarring. Naturally that can create many conflicting thoughts and it is likely that the current and prevalent associations will take precedence and distract you from the spiritual mindset you spent ten months constructing. As I stressed in a previous section on the need to keep your room a sanctuary, the need for timeout to contemplate life and the future to make sure you are not veering off of the spiritual path, is crucial. Hashem, in His infinite kindness, provided us with a weekly outlet by dedicating a day to focus on spirituality. Indeed, by prohibiting activities that may contribute to the distractions of life, He directed our attention to more lofty thoughts. No matter how busy a schedule you possess during the week, Shabbos should be dedicated to your spiritual growth. Whether you go to shul, attend local *shiurim* or read an inspiring book or article, make sure that the focus of your weekly Shabbos experience is saturated with spiritually oriented activities. It may be your last resort and saving grace in maintaining and hopefully, inspiring, further spiritual growth.

> Gila attributed some of her growth in Israel to her numerous Shabbos experiences. From visiting relatives she never knew existed, meeting incredible families that were often both poor (financially) and rich (in happiness and depth), parents engaging their children at the Shabbos table with divrei Torah and with moral conundrums, enjoying the camaraderie with friends at seminary, to spending a Shabbos in Tzfas, to say she developed a new appreciation for Shabbos would be an understatement. It was Gila's ultimate goal to try to replicate those Shabbos experiences in the home she planned on building with her future husband. Nevertheless, for the time being, she would take that newfound appreciation for Shabbos and utilize it to the best of her abilities to gain the most out of her Shabbos experiences upon her return home.

GETTING PRACTICAL

- No matter how busy your week is and how little, if any, time you spent on spirituality, make sure to utilize Shabbos to focus on the spiritual side of life.
- Learn a *sefer*, attend shul and *shiurim* and don't forget to spend time with family.

Rabbinic Counsel

"Make for yourself a Rav."

(YEHOSHUA BEN PRACHIA)[18]

"The more counsel the more understanding."

(HILLEL)[19]

A key aspect to navigating life, overcoming challenges, and avoiding mistakes is to have a rabbinic figure (Rabbi or Rebbetzin) to turn to for advice and direction. No matter how many friends one may have or how aligned one is with their parents and community, a person would do well with having an outside, objective opinion from someone who is not only intelligent and logical, but someone with halachic expertise and steeped in Torah *hashkafah*.

We are all presented with challenges throughout life; sometimes the challenges are rather small, while other times they are quite large. Having someone to consult with that can provide a Torah point-of-view on what to do and how to proceed is crucial in succeeding in

---

18   *Pirkei Avos* 1:6.

19   *Pirkei Avos* 2:8.

life. Now that you are moving onto the next stage in life, the more important this idea becomes.

It is crucial that you find a local rabbinic figure to discuss matters with; someone who will understand your surroundings and can appreciate your background. It is not advisable to solely rely on rabbinic figures from Israel since many times it may be difficult to get in touch with them and sometimes you will need an immediate response. Moreover, given the different society they are in, despite their best intentions, they may not fully understand the dynamics of the society you are in.

Some people may argue that turning to a rabbinic figure for advice for everything you do, removes your independence and freedom to choose. Obviously, the circumstances and the particular question will ultimately determine whether outside counsel is needed. I am not advocating only making decisions with outside rabbinic insight. A responsible and well-informed person generally can figure out where there is halachic uncertainty or the need for *hashkafic* guidance to warrant discussing the matter with a rabbinic figure. Nevertheless, if one is uncertain, erring on the side of caution and asking for advice would be a wise choice.

Seeking advice from a rabbinic figure provides further, and perhaps deeper, perspectives on a particular situation. One does not need to be robotic in following everything they hear from a Rabbi that is not a halachic directive. It gives them another perspective at viewing a situation and opens their mind to alternative positions. Can one get alternative perspectives from another person? They certainly can, but a perspective from someone with a Torah-steeped background adds a more spiritual flavor to the decision-making process, which is crucial; especially with the greater focus you now have for spirituality and the greater appreciation you may have developed for Torah guidance.

> *Upon returning home from Israel and heeding the advice of her teachers in seminary, Shira immediately embarked on a process of finding a rabbinic figure she could look to for advice and consultation. There was no concern for friction evolving in her family due to her change in* hashkafah *as they were all*

pleased with how her Israel experience had panned out and how she had matured as a person. Nevertheless, Shira felt it would be beneficial to have an outsider to look to and consult with regarding handling challenges as they arose. It proved to be of great benefit once she started dating as many questions arose that she was unsure of how to handle. Having a rabbinic figure to look to for advice in what to look for in a boy and what concerns were valid, greatly enhanced her dating experience and assisted Shira in finding her bashert.

GETTING PRACTICAL

- Find a Rav and/or Rebbetzin locally that you feel comfortable with that you can ask questions and seek advice from.
- Ask for recommendations from friends or people you trust if you do not have a preference for a specific rabbinic figure.

College

"A thorough knowledge of the Bible is worth more than a college education."
(THEODORE ROOSEVELT)

Whether you are a career-oriented individual and believe in the need for higher education for professional reasons, plan on living a *kollel* lifestyle, or believe in higher education simply to become more educated and knowledgeable, most young women returning from seminary continue their secular studies, in one form or another. Higher education can indeed bring many blessings to life, but there are many pitfalls and potentially dangerous situations that one can encounter in a university or college setting that must be accounted for, especially at a secular institution.

It may be your first encounter with coeducational experiences and the presentation of ideas and studies that are contrary to Jewish and Torah-based beliefs. If you are not properly prepared, it will be easy for you to stumble and lose your spiritual bearings.

Although Lauren wanted to attend a college without having to sit with the opposite gender in the same classroom, financial considerations and familial pressures compelled her to attend the local coeducational school. Lauren had changed a lot over the past year having spent a year abroad in seminary where she found the depth of Torah study and all the background behind the laws and customs to be fascinating and surprisingly relevant even in today's modern times. She had gained a greater appreciation for Judaism and the role of women and was excited to implement some changes in her life that she felt would conform better to what the Torah had in mind.

Lauren had grown up attending the local day school that separated classes by gender starting in fifth grade so this would be her first time in a coeducational environment at a mature age. She was not really concerned about it given her new perspectives on life and figured she would do her best to focus on the education part and avoid any distractions or extracurricular activities. Unfortunately, she did not realize the difficulty in doing that. She had never been pursued by boys before, and now in every class it seemed at least one was trying to befriend her. In truth, she kind of liked the attention she was receiving.

One of the main problems was that the young men that were approaching her were not the types she envisioned marrying and spending the rest of her life with. Many were not even Jewish! She didn't feel that she could ignore them or push them away because the attention was very flattering — and she did not think there could be much harm in talking to someone she would never marry.

Another problem Lauren encountered was the mode of dress common in her new environment. She identified with the spirit and rules of tznius *and it was hard to discount the fact that the secular girls looked more attractive by revealing more than she was and wearing more tightly fit clothing that accentuated their slim figures. The fact that some of the males were "joking" about her mode of dress and encouraging her to dress more like everyone else was certainly not helping the situation. Lauren couldn't look for encouragement from her family since they were not too excited about her new-found "religiosity." Lauren was in a bind and was having a very difficult time holding on to the changes she implemented into her life.*

Some may not be concerned with what happened to Lauren since they live in a large Jewish community and even if they attend a coeducational school, they will have many other observant Jews attending school with them, so that the pressures to conform will be severely reduced. They may be right to an extent, depending on one's perseverance and associations, but we are all influenced by what we hear and see. It is impossible not to be impacted and influenced by our surroundings.

Other issues can arise that may directly or indirectly steer you off of the straight and narrow path. Taking classes in philosophy or the sciences where professors are teaching agnostic or atheistic ideas on a consistent basis can influence one's thinking and beliefs, even for those who believe they are prepared for it.

Many yeshivah boys and seminary girls change over the course of their college attendance. You may not be able to avoid attending such institutions for whatever legitimate reasons, but be prepared! After all, some get stronger spiritually while in secular surroundings — it can be done!

GETTING PRACTICAL

If you will be attending a secular institution,

- Try to limit your exposure and time there.
- Stay close to other Jews that are there.
- Avoid classes that may teach heretical ideas or subjects that may be contrary to Torah-true Jews.

Internet

"Getting information off of the internet is like taking a drink from a fire hydrant."

(MITCHELL KAPOR)

The internet reminds me a little bit of the *parah adumah*. The *parah adumah* was a paradox in that it was used to purify those that were defiled, but it also defiled those who were pure and came into contact with it.

The internet, in a similar vein, provides a lot of good and positive information, but there are also significant negatives to it, depending on what it is ultimately used for. One can pretty much find anything he/she needs on Judaism from lectures, classes, *divrei Torah*, and *halachos* to how-to videos. If one wants to find out the name of a relative of a certain biblical figure such as Avraham Avinu's mother's name, for example, one can Google it and discover the answer within seconds (Amaslai). Who needs *seforim* anymore? There are certainly negatives to that convenience as well, but there are more serious negatives as well.

The most well-known issue with the internet is the accessibility of pornography and other inappropriate forums. Although this may be a greater issue for the male population than for the female population, it is not only a male issue. In terms of watching or viewing this type of stuff, don't get anywhere close — the damage is horrible.

Nevertheless, I believe a more common and therefore serious issue with the internet is the availability of misinformation on every topic, especially the Torah and Judaism. Anyone who has questions about Judaism or the Torah and believes he has discovered inconsistencies within the Torah and searches online can find blogs or websites that vindicate and exacerbate the questions — and may lead one to believe that there truly is a problem and inconsistency with the Torah and Judaism.

In truth, all these questions have been answered and every question can be answered, but if you look to the wrong sources for a response, it can lead one down a path of no return.

With all the challenges in life today and the difficulties in leading a healthy and happy lifestyle, the inclination toward base desires and the removal of any burden that hinders one's ability to access those desires, is prominent and pervasive. When the going gets tough, the natural inclination of a person may be to remove oneself from the difficulty at hand, even for a brief reprieve. A person dealing with hardships or challenges that appear too difficult to bear, or a person who just wants to escape from "real life" for a few hours, may look to the internet for that reprieve. In doing so, he/she may peruse things that provide instant gratification to get one's mind off of the issue at hand. Alternatively, one may be more attracted to heretical ideas or writings that challenge strict observance of Judaism since the removal of restrictions would appear to ease some of the pressure the person is dealing with. When faced with many challenges, a Jew may look to free himself from all the legal burdens imposed on him by his religious observance rather than deal with the other difficulties he is managing that cannot be resolved or removed as easily. In other words, the internet is an easily accessible medium that can provide relief to someone under pressure who may not be strong enough to withstand the negative influences he may come across or is drawn to.

There are so many ways for one to be distracted online from spiritual pursuits between the waste of time in web surfing, viewing inappropriate images and videos, and reading heretical material, that the internet can completely engulf and take over one's life. It is a great tool for the *yetzer hara* to posses — and most probably the most effective tool he has ever had. Like many things in life, there are positives to the internet, but one must be very careful in navigating the waters to only utilize this tool for benefits that do not hamper one's spiritual makeup.

If one is going to use the internet, it should be with a filter and preferably with a buddy system as well. Thus, any inclination toward something inappropriate would be diffused immediately. My company requires me to have a laptop and access to the internet at home. In order to protect myself, I had a filter installed and my Rav is my buddy; he gets a weekly report of every website I have visited.

GETTING PRACTICAL

- Use a computer in a public area, preferably where people can walk by at any time.
- Install a filter and have a buddy monitor internet access.

Emunah

"Delve into the Torah and continue to delve in it,
for everything is in it."

(BEN BAG BAG)[20]

ince the creation of the internet, the amount of people suffering from a crisis in *emunah* has increased significantly. One can literally find an article online challenging any matter of Judaism or the Torah. Between all the challenges in living an observant lifestyle to begin with, the sad reality of the imperfections of contemporary *frum* life, and the internet induced questions of faith to boot, it is no wonder why so many are having difficulty in maintaining and strengthening their *emunah*. A young lady fresh off of a year in Israel may not be too concerned for such eventualities as it is difficult, if not impossible, to envision such a crisis in *emunah* to evolve given her current spiritual status. Nevertheless, you are inevitably going to experience situations that are either directly relevant to you or just something you read or view from afar, that will affect your beliefs and compel you to question your life goals and whether your pursuits are legitimate.

I would once again encourage you to look to a rabbinical figure for guidance. All questions you may have can be answered by someone with the proper knowledge in Torah. No matter what people say or write about the world based on science or other sources, those subjects are always evolving. The only immutable source that has stood the test of time and incessant challenges to its veracity has been the Torah.

A number of years ago, I attended a halachah conference and one of the presenters, Rabbi J. David Bleich, spoke about the halachic status of brain death and whether it is considered death in halachah. One of the thoughts he shared was the following: About 250 years ago, during the life of the Chassam Sofer, society viewed Judaism's custom to bury its deceased members as quickly as possible, to be immoral. The general scientific belief at the time was to wait seventy-two hours after a person "died" in order to make sure he/she was actually deceased. Jews were thought to be burying alive their own members. The Chassam Sofer was adamant in following the Jewish perspective despite the pressures general society placed on the Jewish population at the time. The irony of that position in current times is obvious. Secular society views Jews as being immoral for not pulling the plug on its members who are brain dead and allowing them to "suffer." Society believes that brain death is a definitive determinant of death and Jews are vilified as being immoral for keeping their own, who are brain dead, alive.[21] The Jewish status of death and handling a corpse has not changed over the last 250 years, but science's position has. And it is likely to evolve further as time goes on.

Unfortunately, we may fall prey to the seemingly intellectual arguments on religion and other matters due to society's views of science and medicine as superior to any other source. Additionally, when dealing with a crisis or two in one's own life, one may be more vulnerable to accepting and believing the lies and deceit that are pervasive online and accessible to anyone searching or who happen to come across while browsing. One must keep in mind that Judaism has the answers even if you are not familiar with the answers. All

---

21   Every situation is different and one must consult with his halachic authority for guidance.

you need is to find the right person well-versed enough to explain to you whatever conundrum or question you may have.

GETTING PRACTICAL

- No matter what secular arguments or perspectives you come across, always remember that the only immutable position is that of the Torah.
- Look to a rabbinic figure for guidance when you are suffering from a question of faith.

Dating

"Single isn't a status, but it's a word that describes a person who is strong enough to live and enjoy life while searching for a suitable marriage partner."

(ANONYMOUS)

D ating is likely going to be prominently on your mind soon after you arrive home, if not sooner. I would like to share an observation with you: I have noticed that many girls who date for a while and do not get married within a couple of years of dating, appear to experience greater difficulty in maintaining their spiritual elevation. One can speculate as to the reasons behind such a regression, whether it is a getting-back-at-G-d kind of a response or related to feelings of depression, but the phenomenon is common. The key is that you prepare for the possibility that you may not get married right away and accept the situation. Hashem has a plan for everyone and for some, staying single longer than others is part of the individualized plan specifically designed for them. Preparing for potential challenges can help in allaying some of the anxiety and depression that may arise from facing such a challenge. Nevertheless, I am not attempting to minimize the difficulty of the challenge. You must keep in mind that challenges are sent our way to strengthen the bond we have with Hashem, not to weaken the bond.

Whatever the circumstances you may find yourself in, try to make the most of it and enjoy the benefits associated with it. I am reminded of an older single who attended law school with me; she used to lament her status and inability to find her *bashert*. I tried to encourage her to enjoy the independence and lack of responsibility while it lasted, but she never seemed to accept that. Years later, after she married and bore children, I encountered her and she confided that she regretted not heeding my advice.

Speaking to others in the same boat as you — dealing with the same challenge — can provide support and a crutch to lean on. It can encourage one to face the challenge head-on and overcome it with the knowledge that others are "there" with you. Keep in mind that the longer the process takes and the greater the difficulty, the more rewarding it will be and the greater the appreciation you will have for your spouse when, G-d willing, you do meet your *bashert*. And that should not be taken for granted and minimized in one's mind. Although it would be nice to be set up with your *bashert* on the first try — and no one desires for the process to be long and difficult — every chapter in one's life must be analyzed and appreciated on its own merits. Some things will come relatively easy while others will be more difficult. The key is your attitude and how you deal with the challenges.

GETTING PRACTICAL

- As with everything in life, understand that some things come easier than others.
- Appreciate the process. Any difficulties that come along with it are there to make you stronger.

Marriage

"Behind every great man is an even greater woman."

(ANONYMOUS)

Belonging to the male gender, I have always been amazed at the prominence and pervasiveness of the concept of marriage on the minds of the female gender. From little toddlers playing out wedding scenes with their dolls to teenagers and post-seminary girls constantly discussing the topic, it appears to be of ultimate inherent importance. And in all honesty, having been married for over a decade and observing the incredible potential that can be fulfilled by the right partnership of male and female, I can understand it — to the extent my male-slanted mind will allow.

Aside from their own "direct" *avodas Hashem*, with Hashem having created the female gender with more of an innate connection to Him, one of their amazing abilities is to bring out the potential and latent spiritual talents of their husbands. For example, aside from her continuing to attend a weekly Torah class, when she encourages him to learn, a woman shares in his reward (and doesn't get penalized when he wastes time![22]).

---

22   See *Berachos* 17a and *Michtav Me'Eliyahu*. I also heard the same idea in lectures from Rabbi Yosef Viener and Rabbi Yisroel Reisman, quoting a *shiur* heard from Rabbi Gedalia Schorr.

Marriage is an exciting endeavor, and potentially the greatest chapter in one's life. It can and should bring out the best of each partner. Still, it also offers challenges to each that they did not incur previously — and would not encounter — if not for the partnership. As such, although the goal is to help each other grow and bring out the potential of one another, it can also have the opposite effect of bringing down the other. No matter how similar their backgrounds are and the parallel lives they lived up until this point, there are going to be differences that arise from living with someone new for the first time. They may be of insignificant importance or of minor halachic consequence; in either case, if you are not mature enough and prepared to deal with the situation, it can spiral into much greater controversy with irreversible ramifications.

It is interesting to note that the two most important "exercises" one will engage in, in life, are marriage and raising children — and most people I know do not look to significantly educate themselves in preparation for those exercises. (Although, over the past number of years marriage courses have become more common.) Having spent the last ten months engaged in rigorous Torah study and self-growth and improvement, you are better equipped to handle and deal with life's challenges, including those that are brought on by marriage.

Nevertheless, without continued focus on growth and maturity, it is not difficult to falter in such exercises. Once again, having a Rav or Rebbetzin to talk to and engage in discourse to guide you in the proper way of dealing with challenges that arise is crucial. Without having an objective, wise individual with Torah-steeped *hashkafah* to look to for advice on matters of life and all challenges that may arise, it would be difficult, if not impossible, to succeed in life's most important endeavors. It is always better to seek advice, even on simple matters, than to approach a matter without any forethought or blindly without any input from an objective outsider. After 120 years when coming before the heavenly tribunal, if one always engaged the advice of a rabbinic figure, no one can fault you and no prosecution can be brought against you since you were following the dictates of what the Torah wanted you to do. It is a failsafe method to protect your position in the heavenly tribunal — who wouldn't want such a support?

There is one more idea I would like to discuss: Throughout Tanach (see Preface) there are many well-known instances of where a woman saved her husband from inevitable doom, or merely advised him of the error of a decision he was going to make. Sarah Imeinu was correct in advising Avraham Avinu to evict Yishmael from their house because of the potential negative impact he could have on Yitzchak Avinu. Rivkah Imeinu saw through the deception of Eisav, despite Yitzchak Avinu's belief to the contrary, and correctly advised Yaakov to deceive Yitzchak Avinu in order that Yaakov would receive the *berachos* instead of Eisav. Such advice and persuasions not only saved the husband from a bad decision, but many times saved his life and the life of others (both physically and spiritually).

The point is: be involved with your husband and be aware of all his actions and endeavors. I am not advocating that you be his "worst nightmare" — his *mashgiach* on call 24/7 — that isn't the way to start married life together!

Still, a wife should know what her husband is doing in his profession, monitor his internet access, and know who he is acquainted with and spending time with outside of the house. Like everyone, male or female, your husband will have a *yetzer hara* to contend with and it will look to attack and engage his interest in inappropriate matters. There have been too many men caught engaging in unethical business practices and using the internet for inappropriate matters. It is impossible to monitor and be on top of him all the time and if you attempt to do so, it will destroy your marriage and the trust you have in each other.

Nevertheless, with regard to matters you can monitor well without having to appear too nosy, you need to be on top of; particularly, internet access and use. It has become common in observant Jewish households to have software monitoring services that prevent inappropriate images from appearing on the screen and restrict access to inappropriate websites. Additionally, many people have software that allows for a computer to be monitored by a third party, someone one can trust in issuing discipline when necessary and someone the computer user will be fearful of should he see inappropriate websites being accessed or visited. As I noted earlier in the chapter on the internet, I personally have my Rav as my partner and he is aware of every single website I visit on my computer.

If you have a husband that is a blogger or engaged on social media, it is important for you to be aware of what he is writing and doing on those websites. There are many blogs and articles that I have come across and wonder if the authors' spouses are aware of what they are writing. In many cases, I believe the spouse would be able to deter and change the position of the author, who many times is writing things that are antithetical to Torah-based Judaism and are having a significantly negative impact on readers.

I know a world-renowned Rav who recently started using e-mail and shares the same e-mail address with his wife so that she can be aware of all his e-mail correspondence. Another Rav I know, who writes magazine articles, always has his wife proofread and give him suggestions. This same Rav will also not speak to any female privately without his wife in the room. I recall once taking my mother to speak with my Rebbi and he would not close the door when speaking to my mother, despite the fact that I was waiting right outside the door. My point being, don't feel immature or in violation of some marriage code by monitoring the internet access and content exposure of your husband. No one is immune to the *yetzer hara* and without the assistance of one's spouse, just as in many areas of life, one will be more prone to failure. Many things can only be conquered, and one will only merit success, with the assistance of their spouse.

The ideal marriage partnership is for each spouse to constitute two halves of a whole. There is a well-known story of Rabbi Aryeh Levine visiting a doctor with his wife, who was suffering foot pain, and he told the doctor that "our" foot hurts. They had reached the level of oneness together.

Rabbi Moshe Feinstein[23] explains that there are very few righteous women discussed in Tanach because most of them became great through

---

23   See *Darash Moshe, Parashas Vayigash*, as heard from Rabbi Yisroel Reisman.

their partnership with their husbands. We don't know anything about the wives of the *shevatim* or Shmuel HaNavi (and they likely were righteous women having been married to such great people), for example, because they were one with their husbands. In the manuscripts found from Rav Yehudah HaChassid on Chumash, he explains that the reason the Chumash only mentions three women (Dina, Serach, and Yocheved) as part of the seventy people that went down to Egypt with Yaakov Avinu is because they were not married. It wasn't that sixty-seven of the people were male and there were only three females (talk about a *shidduch* crisis!), but rather many of those males were married and had achieved oneness with their wives. Most of the righteous women mentioned in Tanach are there because they had achieved greatness prior to marriage; they were already great independent of their husbands.

The following story is related about Rabbi Yosef Chaim Sonnenfeld. He was sitting at a table with his wife and commented that when he comes to the *Olam HaEmes*, they will reveal him to be the fraud that he is. Rabbi Yosef Chaim was stating that he was not as great of a person as people thought he was. Then he told his wife that she did not have to be concerned, since she conducted herself like a person married to a great individual, and will thus be judged to be great herself. She responded that she will not agree to enter Gan Eden without her husband. He, in turn, responded that that is precisely what he is banking on to earn entry into Gan Eden — his wife.

Every woman has the ability to bring her husband to Gan Eden with her. It is a great responsibility, but a tremendous achievement for those who accomplish it.

GETTING PRACTICAL

- Be aware of what your husband is doing.
- Positive encouragement can go a long way in helping him overcome his *yetzer hara*.

Tefillah

"Do not forget the Rock Who has engendered you and given you life, know Him in everything you do, and keep Him constantly in your thoughts."

(RABBEINU ASHER)[24]

A s I was preparing to depart from Israel upon the conclusion of my time in yeshivah, my Rosh Yeshivah brought me into his office to give me a talk. Honestly, I do not remember much of the content of his talk to me fifteen years ago, but one message resonated with me and has stuck with me ever since. His lasting message to me was to appreciate the importance of *tefillah* and to utilize it effectively. I had a number of personal challenges throughout my year in Israel that the Rosh Yeshivah was aware of and he was reminding me to maintain a *kesher* with Hashem and utilize the great gift of *tefillah* to connect with Him.

According to the Rambam,[25] it is a mitzvah from the Torah to perform

---

24   *Orchos Chaim*, Chapter 4, Verse 21.
25   See *Mishneh Torah, Hilchos Tefillah*, Chapter 1.

tefillah daily.[26] The Gemara[27] tells us that *tefillah* is composed of words that ascend to the heavens and is among those things that stand at the pinnacle of creation. Nevertheless, *tefillah* is only as effective as we make it. *Tefillah* is referred to as the *avodah she'baleiv*. The potency of our *tefillos* depends on the intention and feelings within our hearts.

Sometimes, in His ultimate kindness, Hashem sends us challenges in order to invoke greater concentration and produce more heartfelt *tefillos*. When we beseech Hashem, we are recognizing and acknowledging the fact that it is only He Who can help us.

Life provides a number of ups and downs as one navigates its path. The best way to "steer the boat" and overcome the waves of distractions and challenges, is to maintain a connection to our Father in Heaven. No matter what difficulties you encounter, remember that they are there to help you grow and to strengthen your connection to Hashem. Hashem does not send challenges we cannot overcome. Nevertheless, there are times when the world seems to be caving in on us without any solution in sight. If there was one message I wanted to leave you with, it would be to always keep a connection to Hashem. He is always listening to what we have to say and always responds to our requests. The answer may be "no," but that just means what we were requesting was not good for us, as our Creator knows what is best for us — better than we can ever know.

GETTING PRACTICAL

- Make sure to set time daily to daven.
- Try reciting *Tehillim* daily as well. Understanding what you are reading can be very inspiring.
- No matter what life has in store for you, do not neglect your connection with Hashem.

---

26   See "Pray with All Your Heart — A Guide to More Meaningful *Tefillah*," by Rabbi Shaya Cohen.

27   See *Berachos* 6b.

Epilogue[28]

"In the middle of difficulty lies opportunity."

(ALBERT EINSTEIN)

A great example of the extremes one can attain depending on the path they choose to pursue is illustrated by the differing paths Rus and Orpah ultimately chose. After the sudden and untimely deaths of their husbands, Naomi attempted to persuade both Rus and Orpah to return home to their royal Moabite families rather than continue on to Eretz Yisrael and live a life of poverty. The choices each one made demonstrate the differences between them.

Rus elected to cling to Naomi and pursue a spiritual life, despite the hardships it may entail and in fact, Rus experienced difficulties that most would not be willing to bear.

At the other extreme, Orpah (despite initially following Naomi, as Rus did) eventually returned home. The *pasuk* in *Megillas Rus* relates that she kissed Naomi farewell.[29] Chazal say that whenever Tanach uses a form of the word *neshikah*, "kiss," there is an element

---

28   Most of the material in this section was originally heard in a lecture by Rabbi Yisroel Reisman on *Megillas Rus*.

29   1:14.

of insincerity in that act — aside for one instance: when Orpah bid Naomi farewell.[30]

Nevertheless, despite all the spirituality she absorbed while in a Jewish environment and her initial willingness to continue to pursue a spiritual lifestyle, the Midrash states that on that very night, Orpah degraded herself terribly and Golias was conceived that night as a result of her actions.[31]

How is such extreme, depraved behavior possible after being married to one of the generation's *tzaddikim* (as Chazal point out about Machlon and Kilyon[32]), and spending all that time with Naomi?

Rabbi Chaim Shmuelevitz in *Sichos Mussar* explains that the higher one rises, the harder the fall is, if and when it occurs.[33] A piece of glass on the floor will not experience as much damage when impacted as a glass that falls to the floor. Because Orpah experienced such a spiritual uplifting, the fall from grace was that much greater.

The events of Rus and Orpah should be an example of what may transpire for young women returning home from seminary. Those who cling to the elevated spiritual attainments they achieved must understand that such a lifestyle can be very difficult and challenging at times — just as Rus experienced. She got married to Boaz, conceived, and he passed away that very night.[34] She remained a widow while raising her child and was subjected to questions on the status of her conversion for generations to come. As a matter of fact, it was still debated in the times of David HaMelech, as there were those who believed David could not be king because of his lineage, i.e., Rus's questionable conversion.[35] Rus was still alive at the time (she had a seat next to Shlomo HaMelech's throne[36]) and had to endure all those challenges. Nevertheless, she overcame it all and was rewarded greatly with an exceptionally long life and being the mother of the ancestral line to Mashiach.

---

30   See *Yalkut Shimoni* on *Rus.*
31   Ibid.
32   See *Bava Basra* 91a; *Rambam, Hilchos Melachim* 5:9.
33   Ibid.
34   See *Yalkut Shimoni, Rus.*
35   See *Rashi* on *I Shmuel* 17:55.
36   See *I Melachim* 29; *Bava Basra* 91b.

On the other hand, the tremendous and rapid decline of Orpah should be a grave warning to those who do not protect themselves from the potential pitfalls that may evolve from a lack of spiritual protection. The result of falling from the spiritual high of the Israel experience can be so grave, as Orpah demonstrated, that one can descend far greater than had they never enjoyed the Israel experience.

The higher one reaches and attains throughout his/her time in Israel, the greater the potential fall can be. Chazal implemented many safeguards and restrictions in halachah to protect against violations of Biblical laws based on human nature. You must take that as an example and implement safeguards to protect against the potential pitfalls that are inevitable. Knowing yourself and your weaknesses, you can certainly prepare and avoid such scenarios as much as possible.

That being said, you can indeed lead a wonderful, spiritual life! Follow in the footsteps of Rus and you can change the world and make a huge impact. Just as she merited becoming the progenitor of Mashiach, you, too, can be rewarded handsomely.

It is Rus (and all the other female heroines in Tanach) whom you should strive to follow, and with that honor, may we merit seeing the ultimate redemption and the arrival of Mashiach, speedily in our time.